D0331408

Design Director: Bill Johnson
Cover design by Justin Evans

Library of Congress Cataloging-in-Publication Data:
An application to register this book for cataloging has been submitted to the Library of Congress.
International Standard Book Number: 978-1-59979-726-7

First Edition

09 10 11 12 13 — 987654321
Printed in the United States of America

This book is dedicated to you.

You may have just reached the end of the worst day of your life. You may be desperate for answers but hearing none. It's not by accident that you picked up this book. This story of a man who experienced the worst day of his life three thousand years ago can inspire you with hope for your life today. If you do what David did on his worst day, it is my hope that when you finish, like him you will be able to say:

Why are you down in the dumps, dear soul?
  Why are you crying the blues?
Fix my eyes on God—
  soon I'll be praising again.
He puts a smile on my face.
                    —PSALM 42:11, THE MESSAGE

Contents

FOREWORD

HAVE YOU EVER faced such a great crisis that it left you with a question mark for a brain? There comes a time in everyone's life when you have to confront the unexplainable absences of God, a season in life when God gives no explanations, only promises from His Word. Much of the journey to heaven must be made in the dark. Life is not fair, but God is just. Sometimes all you can trust in is the character of God.

Why do bad things happen to good people? Where is God when I hurt? Everyone is going to have their "dark night of the soul." I've learned that regardless of where I am or what my circumstances are, God is still love, and His grace is sufficient for me.

In this God-inspired book, Brian Zahnd gives you a blueprint for how to survive the worst day of your life. My wife and I have read and reread every word in this book.

It was like God's voice to us in one of the toughest seasons in our lives. I have recommended it to countless people who were facing their own personal Gethsemane. There are some things in life that you cannot escape, but you will live through them. Don't stop because it's dark. Read this book, and follow the proven steps of a man who lost everything but lived to recover it all.

—Jentezen Franklin
New York Times best-selling author of *Fasting*

Preface

I<small>T'S AN UNCERTAIN</small> time, and people are looking for an anchor of hope. People often feel as if they are facing the worst day of their lives. There are always those who, no matter the state of the economy or the stability of the social order, are suddenly face-to-face with unexpected tragedy and are not sure what to do next. Twenty-first-century society is being forced into a strange and unreliable world. People are under a lot of pressure, and they long for a reassuring word. It's for these people that the story of David's calamity at Ziklag and how he eventually recovered is so relevant. A story from three thousand years ago inspires us with hope for today. This is the mysterious capability of God's Word to speak to us in every age.

I distinctly remember the moment of inspiration when I got the idea for this book. My assistant had remarked to me how many people in our church were going through hard times. A few minutes later, I was getting ready to go home for the evening. I paused at the top of some stairs as I thought, "A lot of people are going through hard times."

In a flash of inspiration, I remembered the story of the hard time David went through when he and his fighting men returned to their homes at Ziklag. He had lost everything—his home, his finances, and his family—but that wasn't the end of the story. Miraculously, David found a way to recover all.

Standing at the top of those stairs with my hand on a light switch (I remember it well), I thought, "That must have been the worst day of David's life—but he recovered, and recovered all." That weekend I preached a sermon titled "What to Do on the Worst Day of Your Life." People told me it really helped them, and tapes of this sermon made their way to people around the world. I received letters from people in the Philippines, Mexico, India, Nigeria, and other countries telling me how this message had helped them in times of deep crisis. Others began to encourage me to put this sermon in print.

Finally, in 1997 I printed a few thousand copies of this book and sold them in my church and places where I would preach during my travels. It was no big deal. It's been out of print for years, but I continued to hear reports about this simple little book. Ministries in Russia and India requested permission to translate, print, and distribute it. Almost never a month went by that I didn't hear from someone about how they had been helped by the sermon or the book on what to do on the worst day of your life.

Then in December of 2008, Jentezen Franklin called to tell me how, while going through a difficult period in his life, he had found my little book and had been helped by it. He called to express his gratitude. He was the second person that week who had spoken to me about this eleven-year-old book that had been out of print for years. Jentezen then shared his opinion that the book was timely and should be published, and he asked if I'd mind if he made a few inquiries. I basically shrugged and said, "OK." Suddenly there was a flurry of phone calls and then a mad dash to update the manuscript over the Christmas holidays. This new publication of *What to Do on the Worst Day of Your Life* is the result. I couldn't be more surprised. Yet there may be an explanation.

There are times and seasons to the purposes of God. Occasionally, something can be born out of time. It may be that *What to Do on the Worst Day of Your Life* was originally born out of its time or born ahead of its time. Or perhaps now the time has simply come for it to find a wider audience. In 1993 a lot of people in my church were going through a hard time. Today a lot of people in America are going through a hard time: economic uncertainty, trillion-dollar bailouts, wide-scale layoffs, rising unemployment, massive home foreclosures, and the destructive repercussions from the stress these realities place on families and individuals. And all this is happening in the context of tremendous social, cultural, political, and spiritual change in twenty-first-century America.

The Victory Parade

Recently while in Rome, I walked on the *Via Triumphalis*—the ancient road of the Roman victory parade. Victorious emperors and generals led their armies down this road in a celebration of triumph. The apostle Paul was aware of the Roman victory parade and used it as a prophetic metaphor to describe our life in Christ. In his letter to the Colossian church, the great apostle tells us that we are always being led in the victory parade of Christ. This is the great reality for those who have connected their lives by faith to the Lord Jesus Christ. We are made to share in His victory and are led in His triumphant march.

But it doesn't always seem like it. It doesn't always feel like we are living life in a victory parade. Sometimes life feels more like a death march than a ticker-tape parade. Fortunately, the Bible doesn't ignore this experience or shy away from addressing such realities. The Scriptures don't flinch from telling the stories of hardship and tragedy visited upon the righteous. The overarching storyline of the Bible is *not*, "Once upon a time, they lived happily ever after." Instead, the divine story of God's people has plenty of moments where the narrative, in effect, says, "Then all hell broke loose."

The glorious thing about the chronicles of Scripture is that disappointment is never the end of the story—not for those who believe God. Instead, the barren *do* give birth, the slaves *are* set free, the Promised Land *is* found, the temple *is* built...and rebuilt, Messiah *does* appear, the kingdom *does* come, and the dead *are* raised. And in the story we have before us now, David *does* recover from the worst day of his life. This is why people have loved the Bible for thousands of years—people of every age need hope.

What is found in the story of David and his ultimate recovery from the Ziklag disaster is not just an inspiring story of hope but also a pattern for faith. In this story we find a kind of timeless template for how to make the exceptional choice of faith and encounter God's restorative power in the midst of deep tragedy. So, come with me and see what David did on his worst day. See how David's interface with God's grace was able to bring him into a place of full recovery. We'll see David weep but not get bitter. We'll see David encourage himself and get a word from God. We'll see David reorient his vision and regain his passion. We'll see how David attacked his enemies, recovered all, and celebrated his victory by sharing with others. We'll see how David's worst day was woven into a tapestry of grace in such a way as to become a vital link to God's appointed destiny for his life. All along the journey we'll remember that God's great work in David's life was not an odd, one-off miracle but a pattern of faith for all who are facing the worst day of their life.

David's Worst Day

WHAT DO YOU do on the worst day of your life?

It had been the worst day of David's life.[1] We think it was the year 1012 B.C. and that David was twenty-nine years old. In those twenty-nine years, David had lived a life of adventure. When he was a teenage boy of about fifteen, the prophet Samuel came to his home in Bethlehem and anointed him as the future king of Israel. A few months later, young David was thrust into sudden fame when he killed Goliath, the champion warrior of the Philistines, in the Valley of Elah. After his stunning triumph over Goliath, David left the sheepfolds of his father, Jesse, and became a member of the royal household of King Saul. Saul made David the commander of his armies, and David led the armies of Israel in one victory after another.

As a daring young warrior, David became the national hero of the Israelites, but when the paranoid and neurotic King Saul became jealous of David's tremendous success and popularity and sought to kill him, David was forced to leave the royal household and roam the hillsides of Judea with his mercenary band of six hundred men. For several years David and his men fought the Philistines while expanding and securing the borders of Israel. During this time, as David waited for the fulfillment of Samuel's prophecy that he would be the next king of Israel, David and his men made the city of Ziklag in southern Judea their home.

David and his family, along with David's men and their families, had been living in Ziklag for a year and four months, and not much had transpired. Ziklag was an interim place for David. It was not Bethlehem, the place of his beginning—nor was it Jerusalem, the place of his destiny. Ziklag was somewhere in between. We all spend some time in Ziklag—it's not where we came from, nor is it where we are going; it's just where we happen to be for a while. Ziklag is the place of patient waiting located somewhere between prophecy and destiny. For David, life in Ziklag had been very uneventful, very ordinary, almost boring. Then it happened...

David and his men had been away for a few days in Aphek, a three-day journey from Ziklag, but now they were returning home. All of the men were eager to be home again, to see their wives and children, and to enjoy the comforts of home. As they drew near to Ziklag on the third day, their conversation was light and happy, and their hearts were filled with an eager anticipation of being home soon. But as they drew near to the city, they noticed ominous columns of black smoke rising from the horizon. Their conversation stopped, and their pace quickened as anxious thoughts raced through their minds. As the men rushed toward Ziklag, anxiety gave way to panic as the calamity that had befallen their city came into view.

As the men entered the gates of Ziklag, they were horrified at what they saw. The city had been attacked, ransacked, and set on fire. Every home and every building had been reduced to a smoldering heap of rubble. Through the broken sobs of a few survivors, David was able to piece together what had happened. A raiding band of several thousand Amalekites riding on camels had attacked the city. They looted the wealth of the city, took the women and children captive, and then set the city on fire. As swiftly as they had come, they were gone, taking with them fortunes and families and leaving Ziklag in ashes.

This was the worst day of David's life. Think about how bad this day must have been. In one day David lost it all. His possessions were stolen, his house was burned down, and his family was kidnapped.

We have all had bad days, but have you ever gone bankrupt, watched your house burn to the ground, and had your family kidnapped by terrorists—*all in one day*? Yet this is exactly what happened to David on what must have been the worst day of his life. It raises this question: *What do you do on the worst day of your life?* Thank God that in David's response to the Ziklag disaster we find a pattern for full recovery.

First we must come to grips with Ziklag. Ziklag—the interim place between prophecy and destiny—is a hard place to be. When trouble comes swift and cruel like the Amalekites, Ziklag can be (or at least seem like) the worst day of your life. Unfortunately, there is no way we can avoid Ziklag. As surely as God promised that He "made us kings and priests"[2] to "reign in life,"[3] He also takes us through a process of testing and perfecting through our personal *Ziklag experiences.*

Like David, you will visit Ziklag somewhere between your prophecy and your destiny. This does not mean that God is the source of the difficult experiences in life. God did not send the Amalekites to Ziklag—of this you can be quite certain. The evil of a fallen world and the schemes of the evil one (Satan) are the primary sources for human suffering. Nevertheless, God has His purposes, and with a victorious end in mind, He does allow trouble into our lives.[4] It is in facing and triumphing over the great trials of life that you learn what it means to overcome the world and to live as more than a conqueror.[5] The keynote of the Christian life is victory—the victory that flows from the Cross and empty tomb to transform our lives today.[6] Victory is not the absence of trouble. *Victory* is defined as success in a struggle against difficulties and overcoming an enemy. In this life, you will have plenty of opportunities for victory.

Faith is the victory that overcomes—even on the worst day of your life![7] You don't have to be defeated when trouble comes. There are things you can do and a path you can follow that will lead you beyond the fear and heartbreak of initial loss into a place of authentic victory.

As I look at how David responded to the tragedy that befell him at Ziklag, I can identify ten things that David did—things that progressively led to the miracle of David recovering all. David's experience—and, more importantly, his response—provides for us a pattern for turning tragedy into triumph.

I realize every situation is different and every individual is unique. Nevertheless, there are patterns and principles that are timeless and universal. The scriptural record of David's miraculous recovery is not left to us as merely a historical novelty; it is given to us as a pattern to follow. In the Book of Hebrews, we are exhorted to recognize proven leaders and then follow their faith.[8] David is a proven leader whose faith we can follow! So, please allow me to lead you through the amazing story of how David encountered the worst day of his life but eventually recovered all. You will learn how you can do the same things that David did when you face the worst day of your life. Don't abandon hope. All is not lost. There is a way to full recovery.

Weep

As David stood among the smoldering ruins of what had been his home, he wept.[1] As he faced the awful fact that the Amalekites had in one day reduced him to financial ruin, he wept. As he contemplated the terrifying reality that cruel and murderous bandits had kidnapped his family, he wept. All he could do was cry. Hot tears flowed down his face, and heavy sobs made his body convulse. The only outlet David could find for the fear and the anger and the pain that seized his soul was weeping.

David was not alone in his weeping. Six hundred men, all of them strong and valiant soldiers, men who had faced death many times without a hint of fear, now wept openly and uncontrollably. Many of these men were the champions whose heroic deeds would become legendary in Israel. These weren't weak men. These weren't men prone to emotional histrionics. But they couldn't hold back the hot, salty tears, nor did they want to. The biblical narration tells us they wept until they had no more power to weep. Powerful men wept until weeping had drained their power. They cried and cried until they were too tired to cry anymore.

What do you do when trouble hits you so hard that it knocks the wind out of you and makes you feel that it must be the worst day of your life? The first thing you do is to *go ahead and weep.* Stoicism has nothing to do with faith. Living by faith is not living without feelings. Being strong in faith does not make us immune to emotion. Those who live by faith experience emotion like everybody else—they just don't allow emotion to have the last word. God has created us as emotional beings; it is part of our human nature. Emotions are an essential part of experiencing pleasure and joy in life. Those who deny their emotional makeup become people with bland personalities incapable of really enjoying life. To deny true sorrow is also to deny true joy. Having a flat, prosaic personality is not what it means to be a person of faith.

You cannot even worship God without involving your emotions. David, who is depicted in Scripture as a great worshiper of God, was highly demonstrative in his worship. He would sing, shout, and dance in his praise of God. We can involve the full range of our emotions when we worship God. The emotion that proceeds from a deep understanding of God's glory and goodness is filled with spiritual substance and is both vital and valid in worship. It should not be confused with empty emotionalism, which is emotion for emotion's sake.

If you can contemplate the rich salvation accomplished for you through the suffering of Jesus Christ upon the cross and be completely devoid of any emotional response, there is something wrong. God has made us to feel things. We feel joy, we feel peace, we feel excitement, we feel anger, and we feel sadness—this is how God created human beings. To deny these emotions is to deny your humanity. When the troubles of life strike us with particularly cruel blows, it's natural and perfectly acceptable—and perhaps even helpful—to respond with weeping. Weeping is not inconsistent with faith. Some of the greatest giants of faith in the Bible wept:

- Abraham, the father of faith, wept at the death of his wife Sarah.[2]
- When Jacob met his future bride Rachel, he was so overwhelmed that he wept.[3]
- When Joseph was reunited with his estranged brothers, he wept.[4]
- Hezekiah wept when he received the bad report that he would die from his illlness.[5]
- Nehemiah wept over the sad state of Jerusalem.[6]
- Job wept in the midst of his trial.[7]
- The prophet Jeremiah wept over the sins of Israel.[8]

- Peter wept over his failure and betrayal of Christ.[9]
- Paul wept in the middle of his trials.[10]
- John wept during his heavenly visions.[11]
- Even Jesus wept![12]

The weeping of Jesus is a powerful testimony to the fullness of His humanity. There is much sorrow in this fallen world, and men and women have many reasons to weep.

One of our most beloved Christmas carols is "Away in a Manger." Recently, while splitting wood on a subzero day during the Christmas season, I found myself humming the melody as the words circled through my mind:

> Away in a manger, no crib for a bed,
> The little Lord Jesus laid down His sweet head.
> The stars in the sky looked down where He lay,
> The little Lord Jesus, asleep on the hay.
>
> The cattle are lowing, the Baby awakes,
> But little Lord Jesus, no crying He makes . . . *

I stopped right there. Baby Jesus doesn't cry? Of course He does. Like every baby, Jesus cried at birth. Like every baby, Jesus cried when He was hungry. Like every child, Jesus cried when He was hurt or unhappy. The baby Jesus who doesn't cry is the *halo Jesus*—the Jesus depicted so often in religious art. The problem with the halo Jesus is that He is not human.

---

* "Away in a Manger" by John Thomas McFarland. Public domain.

A baby who doesn't cry is not human. A person who doesn't cry is lacking in humanity. Jesus cried. He cried as a baby, as a child, and as a man. He was a man of sorrows, acquainted with grief. Jesus cried. He shed the tears of God.

God in Christ shed tears? This is an astounding acknowledgment. But nothing that is common to man was kept from God in Christ. Not birth, nor death; not trial, nor temptation; not sorrow, nor suffering. And not tears.

Some theologians have argued for the doctrine of *divine impassibility*. This doctrine, which states that God is without passion or emotion, was first developed by early theologians who were heavily influenced by Greek philosophers. It was later adopted by some of the Reformation theologians. Well, I have a bone to pick with these theologians. They have woefully underestimated the Incarnation. Christ is not God *masquerading* as human. The Incarnation is God made *fully* human—and tears are part of the human condition. Thus, in Christ we find not divine impassibility but *divine suffering*. We find the tears of God. These tears are integral to our salvation. For, as Dietrich Bonhoeffer observed, "Only the suffering God can help."* It's interesting to note that as a direct result of the Holocaust, most theologians now reject divine impassibility. Apparently, the notion that God adopts a passive attitude toward human suffering is no longer tenable in light of the horrendous suffering of the Holocaust.

---

* Dietrich Bonhoeffer, *Letters and Papers from Prison* (London: SCM Press, 1967), 361.

It's not the Stoic Greek philosophers who reflect the heart of God, but the weeping Hebrew prophets—not Zeno the Stoic philosopher, but Jeremiah the weeping prophet. The prophets wept because God weeps. Jesus wept because God weeps. The Word became flesh that God might join us in our tears.

Joy Comes in the Morning

Yet, the tears of God are not tears of mere commiseration. These are holy tears that lead to our liberation—liberation from the dominion of sorrow. God in Christ did not join us in sorrow merely as an experiment in empathy. He joined us in sorrow that He might lead us to the joy that comes in the morning. Jesus has entered fully into the new morning of resurrection. The rest of creation groans, eagerly awaiting the promised liberation.[13]

In the meantime, we who suffer are comforted with the knowledge that we are not alone in our suffering. Jesus joined us in our suffering and shed the tears of God. It is in those tears that we will ultimately find joy unspeakable and full of glory.

In the first Advent two thousand years ago, God in Christ joined us in our tears. The Son of God was born in tears, like every baby that has ever been born. In His second Advent, or Second Coming, God in Christ will join us again, this time to wipe away all of our tears!

In the course of my life and ministry, I've had my own nights of weeping. When I was just a young twenty-two-year-old pastor, I wept as a disgruntled man in the church stood in a service and shouted, "Ichabod, Ichabod, the glory is departed," and then led half the congregation to leave the church. Later, there were times when the pressure and stress became so severe that I was reduced to tears during a very difficult multimillion-dollar building project. I wept when I stood in a hospital room with grieving parents as their teenage son was pronounced dead. There have been times of tears still too personal to talk about. I can say with the apostle Paul that I have served the Lord with many tears.

The Bible says there is a time to weep,[14] and that cannot be denied. It would be an added cruelty to deny yourself or others tears in times of tragedy or deep personal pain.

But there is also a time to dry your tears and stop weeping. "Weeping may endure for a night, but joy comes in the morning."[15]

There is a night of weeping, but there is also a dawn of faith. When the morning comes, it is time to stop weeping and start rejoicing in God. If you continue to weep...if you continue to hold on to your grief and sorrow, it will turn into self-pity, which can destroy your faith and prevent you from coming out of your pain and into a place of victory.

It's important to realize there is a perverse weeping that is founded in self-pity and sinful unbelief. Such weeping arouses the anger of God. When the wilderness generation of Israelites were filled with cravings for the meat, fish, cucumbers, melons, leeks, onions, and garlic they used to eat as slaves in Egypt and complained and wept because all they had to eat in the wilderness was the manna God supernaturally supplied to them, "the anger of the LORD was greatly aroused"![16]

Sinful unbelief led the wilderness generation of Israelites to weep in fear and self-pity. This kind of weeping aroused the anger of God. You will never move out of a place of personal misery into a better and healthier place if you become locked into perpetual self-pity—it's one of the most destructive emotional states a human being can indulge in, and it must be resisted. Even when you have encountered the worst day of your life, there comes a time when you have cried enough. Eventually you must tell yourself, "Enough is enough," and make up your mind to cry no more. Never forget that self-pity is deadly. It has the capacity to destroy your faith and lock you in a self-imposed exile that is difficult to escape. The bottom line is you will never change your life by feeling sorry for yourself.

Listen for the Sound of Marching

There is an interesting story in 2 Samuel 5 about the time when David and his army were in the Valley of Rephaim (*rephaim* means "giants"). They were camped under a grove of mulberry trees. In the Hebrew language, the mulberry tree is called the *baka* tree or, literally, "the weeping tree." In other words, when the army of Israel was in the valley of giant trouble, they sat under the weeping trees. That is what we often do when we find ourselves in the valley of big-time trouble—we sit under the weeping tree. But God gave David a strategy to defeat the Philistines in the Valley of Giants. He told David, "When you hear the sound of marching in the tops of the mulberry trees, then you shall advance quickly." If David would follow these instructions, the promise was, "the LORD will go out before you to strike the camp of the Philistines."[17]

I like that! God instructed David to listen for a sound that could be heard above the mulberry trees—a sound that could be heard above the weeping. It was the sound of marching. What was it? I think it must have been the sound of the angels, the armies of heaven, going forth into battle! When all you can hear is the sound of your own weeping, listen with your spiritual ears for the sound of the angels of God marching into your battle to defeat your adversaries. If you will dry your tears and rise up from under your weeping tree, you can march forward into the battle with the angels. There is a way to move from weeping into victory.

I have seen people who have allowed their grief to conquer them. It's sad and tragic. Their faith atrophies as they languish under the weeping trees. They become so absorbed in their own sorrow that they take it on as their new identity. Instead of *passing through* the valley of weeping—they make a decision to take up residence there. Natural sorrow, when indulged for too long, will cause you to develop a dark and morose personality that will attract demon spirits of depression. No matter what tragedy has visited your life, you still have a divine destiny and an eternal purpose in God that have the potential to bring you joy and satisfaction. Don't allow grief to conquer you! You don't have to stay in the sad place where you find yourself right now. It is possible to rise up and take the steps of faith that will carry you toward a better tomorrow.

The Book of 2 Kings tells an amazing story of four lepers outside the gate of Samaria who had suffered more than their share of hard times. They all had an incurable disease. They were separated from their families and friends, and now they were besieged by famine. They could have easily allowed themselves to be conquered by their grief, and few would have blamed them. But instead, they asked themselves one simple question: "Why sit we here until we die?"[18]

These four men weren't just lepers; they were philosophers of a sort. In their miserable plight, they posed a philosophical question to themselves: Why should we just sit here until we're dead? People who have been overwhelmed with sorrow often ask all the wrong questions—questions like: "Why me?" "What did I do to deserve this?" "How much more will I have to endure?" But this was not the question that the four lepers outside the gate of Samaria asked. They simply asked themselves, "Why sit we here until we die?" Of course, this is a rhetorical question designed to reveal the absurdity of inaction and thus spur them to some kind of positive action. They chose to shake off their depression and to rise up from the miserable place where they had been sitting. With hope renewed, they took faltering steps of faith and marched into a better tomorrow. By rising up and moving forward in faith, they not only found a better tomorrow for themselves, but they also brought salvation to a dying city.[19] You can do the same thing. You can rise up out of your miserable situation and begin to move toward a better tomorrow.

On the worst day of your life you will weep. This is inevitable and understandable. David did, and you will too. It's all right to release the poison of pent-up emotional pain through weeping. But remember, although weeping may last for a night, there will come a dawn of faith when you need to stop weeping and start believing. To turn your tragedy into triumph, you will have to go beyond weeping.

Don't Get Bitter

A
s THE SUN began to set and the last smoldering embers of what had once been Ziklag began to die out, the six hundred men of David's army began to dry their eyes and cease their weeping. They began to gather in small groups and talk in hushed whispers. At first, David couldn't hear them, but as their talk grew louder and angrier, David couldn't help overhearing their conversations. Someone said in a voice hoarse from crying, "This is all David's fault, you know. He's the one to blame. It was his decision to go to Aphek and leave Ziklag undefended."

Another said, "I've lost everything. My money is gone, my family is gone, everything is gone. This would never have happened if I hadn't believed all that crazy talk about David being a king."

Finally, one of David's men spoke what others were already thinking: "I say we stone David. He's the one who got us into this mess, and he needs to pay for it. We should just kill him."[1]

David's day had just gone from bad to worse.

The rash words that led to assertions that David should be stoned to death came from men who owed David a great debt. David found them when they were nobodies, and he had transformed these lonely losers into mighty men. Fleeing from the jealousy of King Saul, David had escaped to the cave of Adullam. Soon, "everyone who was in distress, everyone who was in debt, and everyone who was discontented gathered to him." David became the captain over these lonely losers of Adullam.[2]

The future had held little prospect for these men. They were in debt. They were in distress. They were discontented with life. In other words, they were broke, in trouble, and depressed. Then they heard that David, the son of Jesse, the hero who had killed Goliath in the Valley of Elah, was in the cave outside the city. There were rumors that the prophet Samuel had even anointed him as king of Israel. The elite of Adullam couldn't believe this—it was too far-fetched for them. A king in a cave? What would a man with a kingly anointing and a royal destiny be doing in a cave? So, they just laughed it off as ridiculous.

But the lonely losers of Adullam had nothing left to lose.

As the saying goes, "When you've got nothing, you've got nothing to lose." So, they decided to check it out. When they arrived at the cave of Adullam, they found a good-looking young man about twenty-five years old with red hair sitting inside the cave. They asked him, "Are you David, the son of Jesse?"

David said, "I am."

Then they asked him, "Are you the David who killed the nine-foot giant in the Valley of Elah?"

David again said, "I am." And then to prove it, he showed them the legendary sword of Goliath.

They were awestruck. They asked him, "How did you do it? How did you kill Goliath?"

David said, "I did it by faith in Jehovah." They had never heard of such a thing, and when David recognized in these desperate men a desire to know more, he began to teach them.

Day after day David taught these men. Over time, the losers of Adullam were transformed into the mighty men who would be known throughout the land for their courageous exploits. As they followed the son of Jesse, they were changed. They came out of their debt into prosperity. They came out of their distress into peace. They came out of their discontent into purpose. No one had done more for these men than David.

Now David was finding out how fickle people can be, even people he helped immensely. Now they had forgotten all that David had done for them. Now they spoke of stoning David.

What had happened? They had allowed bitterness to infect their souls. The nature of the flesh is to find someone to blame when you are in trouble. Adam blamed Eve, and Eve blamed the serpent, and people have been blaming somebody else ever since. The blame game belongs to a bitter spirit. When trouble hits, the first thing many people do is get bitter and then blame someone else—usually the leader. This is one of the perils of leadership. Often, bitter people target the leader for blame.

Destructive Bitterness

Bitterness does not belong on the road of recovery. When the worst day of your life hits, you cannot afford to get bitter. If you allow trouble to make you bitter, you are in for worse trouble!

A bitter spirit is incredibly destructive. It will spring up and cause trouble, defiling many in its path.[3] Bitterness will cause untold trouble in your life. Unchecked bitterness has the capacity to wreak havoc in your health, in your mind, in your emotions, in your relationships, and in your finances. Bitterness can cause a world of trouble that will defile others around you. A root of bitterness that began with one person has ruined whole families, companies, and churches. If you allow yourself to become bitter because of your troubles, you will only create more trouble for yourself and those around you.

Bitterness begins as a seed of offense. When you are offended, a negative seed is sown in your heart. If you choose to walk in forgiveness, you stay connected to grace, and that seed is eradicated from your heart by the flow of God's grace. The Bible says that if you fail to forgive, you fall short of the grace of God—you are cut off from the grace of God. The seed of offense becomes a root of bitterness.

As I look back on thirty years of ministry, I am aware that bitterness has destroyed more Christian lives than almost anything else. I am personally aware of countless numbers of people who started on the journey with Jesus and have now abandoned it. Most of them could describe a situation when they were hurt, when they felt abandoned, betrayed, let down, or disappointed by others. Many of them would say it was God Himself who hurt them, betrayed them, and didn't answer their prayers as they thought He should. When I hear a person say they are "mad at God," I shudder inside.

When people say, "I'm mad at God," I wonder whom they think it is they are talking about. Are they expecting that God is just a man who should repent for making them mad?[4] The fear of the Lord is the beginning of knowledge. The fear of the Lord is the beginning of wisdom. And the fear of the Lord is where we must begin in our journey with God. If we don't begin with reverence and holy fear as we seek to encounter God, our foundation is faulty. Jesus spoke unflinchingly about the fear of God, reminding us that it is not the person who can kill our bodies we should fear, but the God who has the power to "destroy both soul and body in hell."[5]

God's loving-kindness and mercy are great, but the almighty God is not to be tempted or trifled with. We must always acknowledge that God is sovereign and righteous. We are treading on dangerous ground when we blame God and become bitter and angry at Him for the things that come into our lives.

Jesus taught that it is inevitable that offenses will come our way.[6] You might as well face it—you are going to be offended. It is one of the guarantees of life: death, taxes, and offenses. People will let you down. This is something you can definitely count on.

When the people in Jerusalem saw the supernatural miracles that Jesus did, many believed in Him. But Jesus knew that popularity would not last. Jesus "…knew what was in man."[7] That popularity didn't last. In the end, He was despised, rejected, and crucified. Jesus understood human nature and knew that they would turn against Him in His difficult hour.

If Jesus knew this about the people, why didn't He become cynical and distrusting? It is because He loves us so much. I try to keep this story in mind as I live my life surrounded by people. I want to constantly love people and believe the best about people, even though I know some will let me down. Remember the prayer of Jesus on the cross? He cried out, "Father, forgive them, for they know not what they do." Sometimes you just have to accept the fact that there are times when people simply don't know what they are doing. When we can learn to pray this prayer for others from our heart, we will experience freedom from bitterness and unforgiveness.

I remember praying with a church member who was

involved in an ugly custody battle with her ex-husband. She was struggling with hating him because of the pain he was causing her. I told her she needed to pray for him and to pray the very prayer that Jesus prayed for those who had nailed Him to the cross. I told her to pray, "Father, forgive him, for he doesn't know what he is doing."

She looked at me and said, "But that's the whole point—he *does* know what he is doing! He knows how he is hurting me." Still, the road to recovery requires the hard choice of forgiveness. The truth is that hurting people hurt people. Each one is perpetuating a cycle of revenge, not understanding that the only way out of the vicious cycle of revenge and retaliation is to forgive—to genuinely forgive from the heart, lay the offense down, and seek peace. This is what the man in the custody battle didn't know. In that sense, he didn't know what he was doing. Make up your mind that you will not recycle revenge.

There are many times when people grievously hurt us, cause us pain—and do it intentionally. May God forgive them. Ultimately, they don't know what they are doing. At the same time, we must not forget that sometimes we are the ones hurting others; we are the ones who don't know what we're doing. The law of forgiveness in God's kingdom is immutable: if we want to be forgiven, we must first forgive.

There are also times when we feel pain, feel wronged, feel disappointed, and yet no one has intended to harm us. There are times when our limited understanding causes us to draw conclusions about people, about circumstances, or even about

God that are just inaccurate. We might be overly sensitive. We might be wrongly suspicious of the motive of others. We might become offended with no valid reason to do so.

Choose to Forgive

Be careful of overestimating your capacity to accurately judge a situation. You may or may not have a *good reason* to be offended. Remember, people were offended at Jesus, and it certainly wasn't His fault.[8] What you must do is make up your mind as to what you are going to do when you are offended. As a Christian, you have only one choice: you must forgive. The apostle Paul gave us very clear instructions for how to respond to an offense, giving us the characteristics of a forgiving heart—"put on tender mercies, kindness, humility, meekness, longsuffering; bearing with one another, and forgiving one another."[9]

Forgiveness keeps you in the flow of God's grace, and God's grace will prevent a seed of offense from taking root in your heart. But if you refuse to forgive (and forgiveness is always a choice), you are cut off from the forgiving flow of God's grace. Jesus was clear on this point, warning us that if we refuse to forgive the wrongs of others, God will not forgive our wrongs.[10]

Most Christians know they aren't supposed to live in offense, and so they play a game of redefining terms. I wish I could count the number of times I've heard someone say, "I'm not offended; I'm just hurt!" It's just a matter of semantics— it's all the same thing. You must forgive.

Choosing to forgive is not unrelated to your recovery from your worst days. When you have been offended by a person or an event in life (and these things are inevitable), choosing to forgive may be the thing that saves your life. Never forget that forgiveness is a choice, not a feeling. God doesn't tell us to "forgive and forget." There are some events that happen in life that we will never forget, but they can be so covered by the grace of God as we live out forgiveness that the pain is eventually erased. This is one of the great aspects of the grace of God.

Furthermore, it is often helpful to understand what forgiveness is not—forgiveness is not an abdication of justice. Instead, forgiveness involves deferring justice to God. We choose to forgive those who have wronged us. How God chooses to deal with those who have wronged us is not our concern. By leaving the business of justice in the hands of God (or with those to whom God has delegated matters of justice, such as civil authorities), we are free to attend to what is our business—the business of forgiveness. By doing this, evil doesn't have the last word, and evil is not allowed to define us. This is the greatest accomplishment of forgiveness.

Forgiveness can save your life, and it can keep you on the journey with Jesus. My heart is grieved as I think about so many Christians who are living isolated, bitter lives because they refused to forgive when they were offended. They are no longer in church, they no longer have real joy, and many of them are estranged from their own family members. Instead of offering forgiveness, they nurtured, rehearsed, and told their sad story over and over—first to others, and then only to themselves. Their offense grew into a root of bitterness that eventually sprang up and caused tremendous trouble in their lives.

We need to take very seriously the warning in Hebrews about the dangers of bitterness. The Old Testament likens a root of bitterness to the wormwood plant, which oozes a bitter oil from its drooping leaves.[11] As a pastor, I have seen too many people turn away from God because of a root of bitterness. A root that would cause us to turn away from God is bitter indeed.

Offense and bitterness are behind the first great crime in human society. Cain became offended when God received Abel's sacrifice and rejected his. Abel's sacrifice was acceptable because it was a blood sacrifice, it was a firstfruits sacrifice, and it was offered in faith. Cain's sacrifice was none of these things, so it was rejected. Instead of learning to offer to God an acceptable sacrifice, Cain became offended at God and Abel, and his offense grew into bitterness. God warned Cain of the danger he was in, telling him, "Sin lies at the door. And its desire is for you, but you should rule over it."[12]

Cain did not heed God's warning, and his bitterness grew until he rose up against his brother Abel and committed the first murder. As a result of becoming bitter, Cain brought a curse and more trouble on his life.

Years ago I heard a preacher give a formula for dealing with the inevitable offenses of life. *Don't curse it. Don't nurse it. Don't rehearse it; but disperse it and reverse it.* I like that and have never forgotten it. When you choose to forgive, you disperse the negative effect of bitterness and reverse the curse associated with it.

After the Israelites crossed the Red Sea, they traveled for three days through the desert without finding any water. When they came to the pools of Marah, they found that they could not drink the water, for it was bitter (*marah* means "bitter"). Instead of believing that the God who had split the Red Sea could also provide water in the desert, the people began to murmur and complain. They became as bitter in their souls as the waters of Marah. As the people complained against Moses (as David's men complained against him), Moses cried to the Lord, and the Lord gave him the solution. God showed Moses a tree that, when cast into the waters of Marah, made the bitter waters sweet.[13]

What was that tree that could turn bitter, poisonous waters into fresh, sweet waters? The Book of Proverbs talks about this tree, saying that a "wholesome tongue [literally, a healing tongue] is a tree of life."[14]

If you will chose to speak positive words—words of life, words of healing, words of forgiveness—instead of negative, critical, blaming, complaining words, you can turn your bitter waters sweet. If you don't, you will poison yourself from the bitter waters that flow out of your own heart. The Bible warns us to "keep your heart with all diligence, for out of it spring the issues of life."[15]

You are drinking from the waters that flow out of your

own heart. Make sure they stay sweet. Don't poison yourself with a bitter spirit.

When you encounter the worst day of your life, make sure you don't become bitter. Choose to forgive, and don't let the seed of offense become a root of bitterness. Don't play the blame game. Don't recycle revenge. Extend forgiveness. Speak healing words instead of critical words. If you can avoid bitterness in your bad times, you will hasten your recovery and save yourself a lot of heartache.

Encourage Yourself in God

S DAVID SAT among the ruins of Ziklag and mutinous men spoke of stoning him, he had a choice. David could allow grief and bitterness to conquer him; he could sink into the black hole of depression and give up and quit. Or he could fight back. But before David could fight, he would have to get his strength and courage back. As David looked around him, he saw nothing but discouraged and downcast men. David had no one to encourage him, so he had only one recourse: he "encouraged himself in the LORD his God."[1]

From what we know of David, I think it is very easy to surmise how David went about encouraging himself. David took his harp, retreated to a solitary place, and began to sing songs of praise to God. No doubt David didn't feel like singing, but he did it anyway. To sing was simply a choice that David made.

David didn't sing a sad lament bemoaning his situation. Instead, David sang of the majesty and power of God. He sang of the Creator who had spoken the worlds into existence. He sang of the deliverer who had already given him improbable victories—victory over the lion, victory over the bear, and victory over the Philistine giant Goliath. Through praise and worship, David changed his focus. On the wings of a song his spirit was lifted above his present circumstances into the presence of the One who is high and lifted up. The melodies of David's harp filled the air as the sweet psalmist of Israel sang praises to the God of heaven who transcends human limitation and is forever seated upon the throne of the universe.

The Bible states it very matter-of-factly: "David encouraged himself in the LORD his God." There was nothing about the circumstance that was encouraging, and had David limited his focus to the present circumstance, he would have surely gone into a deep depression. But David encouraged himself *in God*. In times of uncertainty and upheaval, God was David's constant. God was David's constant because God doesn't change. No matter what the circumstances, God is above it all, seated upon the throne of sovereignty and holding the scepter of dominion. Through praise and worship, David changed his focus so that by the eye of faith he beheld *El Shaddai*—the almighty God.

How did David praise God? Maybe he sang Psalm 34. In fact, I would find it hard to believe that this particular song did not come to David's mind as he sought to encourage himself. David had written this psalm just two years earlier when God had delivered him from the Philistine king Abimelech. I can easily imagine David sitting in the ashes of what was once his home with harp in hand singing these words:

I will bless the LORD at all times;
His praise shall continually be in my mouth.
My soul shall make its boast in the LORD;
The humble shall hear of it and be glad.
Oh, magnify the LORD with me,
And let us exalt His name together.
I sought the LORD, and He heard me,
And delivered me from all my fears.[2]

David sang, "I will bless the LORD at all times." All times—good times, bad times, great times, and terrible times. Even on the worst day of your life, God is worthy of praise. David sang praises to God in the middle of burnt-out Ziklag.

David sang. He sang the amazing lyric, "His praise shall continually be in my mouth." This is part of the path to encouragement. When praise is in your mouth, there will be no grumbling, no complaining, and no negative speaking. Praise is the language of faith. If you want to strengthen your faith, begin to praise God.

Then David sang another lyric: "Oh, magnify the LORD with me." What does that mean? What does it mean to magnify the Lord? *Magnify* means "to enlarge or make bigger in perspective." When we magnify something with a magnifying glass, a microscope, or a telescope, we don't change its reality. We don't make the object we are observing any bigger, but we change our perception of it. We cannot make God any bigger than He already is—you can't increase omnipotence, but you can magnify (or diminish) *your perspective* of God. Perspective has everything to do with whether you are encouraged or discouraged.

Make God Bigger Than Your Trouble

Refuse to magnify the devil. Refuse to magnify the trouble. Refuse to magnify the present negative circumstance. Don't analyze your trouble with a magnifying glass—this will only lead to deeper discouragement. Magnify the Lord! Speak of His greatness, His power, His might. Talk about how big and powerful God is! My Nigerian preacher friend Bishop Goddowell Avwomakpa is in the habit of saying, "When you make God bigger, you make your trouble smaller." It's simple but true.

A thousand years earlier, the young but wise Elihu reminded Job (who was facing his own worst day) that God gives songs in the night.[3] That is an encouraging word. In the dark night of the soul, God will give you a song that, if sung, will bring a dawn of faith and encouragement. So, in the dark night of his personal anguish, David sang a song of praise to the God who can make a way where there is no way.

Paul and Silas did the same thing a thousand years later. They had been arrested for the good deed of casting a spirit of divination out of a young slave girl. After a sham of a trial, they were beaten with rods and imprisoned in the innermost dungeon with their feet in stocks. How did they respond? In a most remarkable way. At midnight, instead of despairing and crying themselves to sleep, they sang hymns of praise to God. Paul and Silas made the exceptional choice to encourage themselves by praising God. Luke tells us that while Paul and Silas sang, the other prisoners were listening to them. No doubt they were! I'm sure the prisoners were amazed at such surprising behavior. Truly these men were different—they had something the other prisoners didn't have. They possessed a remarkable faith in their God, and God responded to their remarkable faith by delivering them from the dungeon of despair through a miraculously timed earthquake. "The foundations of the prison were shaken; and immediately all the doors were opened and everyone's chains were loosed."[4]

Paul and Silas were simply following in the tradition pioneered by David when he encouraged himself with songs of praise. Indeed, as David sang his songs of praise, a change came over him. A spark of faith had brought a glimmer of hope, and David could feel himself becoming encouraged. His men noticed the change also. An encouraged man among a multitude of discouraged men will stand out. That's why David was the leader. The leader will always be the one who can encourage himself when everyone else is discouraged. Had someone else encouraged himself instead of David, that man would have become the new leader. The ability to encourage yourself when everyone else is discouraged is an essential attribute of leadership. In the most desperate times, the ability to summon strength through encouraging yourself is the greatest act of leadership. It's the leadership of Abraham Lincoln...of Winston Churchill...of David.

Encouraging yourself in the Lord is part of how you go about recovering your joy—not the shallow, mercurial feeling of happiness, but deep, abiding joy, which can be present even in the midst of sorrow. I know the idea of having joy in the midst of sorrow may seem paradoxical, but truth is in the paradox. If you are going to recover from the worst day of your life, among the first things you have to recover is your joy. In order to defeat you, the devil knows he must steal your joy. Satan is quite aware of the spiritual truth concerning joy revealed in Nehemiah: "Do not sorrow, for the joy of the LORD is your strength."[5]

What the devil is after through excessive grief and lingering depression is your strength—the strength that is found in the joy of the Lord. Peter talks about the devil utilizing a stalking strategy analogous to a lion stalking its prey. The devil "walks about like a roaring lion, seeking whom he may devour."[6] The devil may be like a lion—not as a metaphor for majesty but as an opportunist seeking to prey upon the weak and feeble. Satan does not want a confrontation with strength; he seeks to exploit weakness.

Understanding that the joy of the Lord is the strength of the believer, the devil seeks to steal your joy, thereby reducing you to weakness. This is a primary strategy utilized by the devil to defeat believers. The believer who can retain his joy is destined to triumph in the end. This is a powerful principle. If the devil cannot steal your joy, he cannot ultimately defeat you. The moment David began to encourage himself in the Lord and recover his joy, he placed himself on a trajectory to turn his whole situation around. Joy is not just a preferred emotional state; it is a necessary element in attaining full recovery.

Think Yourself Happy

The apostle James was the first pastor of the first church. He spent his life in pastoral ministry, and from his experience he was well equipped to give counsel on how people should respond when facing a trial. In the first chapter of his epistle, James gives some vital information about how we are to respond in the midst of a trial. He said we are to "count it all joy when you fall into various trials, knowing that the testing of your faith produces patience." If we allow patience to have its perfect work, we will "be perfect and complete, lacking nothing."[7]

James teaches us that the redeemed should respond to the trials of life completely differently than those who do not have a Christian perspective on life. James teaches us that when we encounter trials, we should "count it all joy." This is a reaction that is definitely counterintuitive but part of the Christian distinctive. The word translated "count" is *hegeomai*. It is an accounting term that means we are to place trials in the joy column of our emotional ledger. We can only do this if we understand the divine purpose behind trials. *Hegeomai* also means "to rule or exercise authority." In fact, *hegeomai* was used to refer to an imperial governor.[8] In other words, when you are thrust into a trial, you must become the governor of your emotions and not allow them to run out of control. You must take authority, rule over your feelings, and choose joy as your dominant emotion. Govern your emotions; don't let them govern you.

The apostle Paul uses the word *hegeomai* when he says, "I think myself happy."[9] Paul was in a trial—literally. He was standing in chains before King Agrippa, charged with insurrection (a crime he did not commit). Insurrection was a capital crime, and Paul's life was at stake in this trial. Paul opened his defense with the words "I think [*hegeomai*] myself happy." In other words, Paul was saying, "I account myself happy. I rule myself happy. I govern myself happy." In spite of his trial, Paul commanded his emotional state to be one of joy and happiness.

On more than one occasion, I have stood in the ruins of Caesarea where Paul made his bold confession, "I think myself happy." I have stood where Paul stood as an accused criminal, bound with chains, and I have thought, "If Paul can make that confession in his great trial, so can I." So, I emulate the faith of Paul. When I find myself in a trial, I think of that judgment hall in Caesarea, and I say, "I think myself happy." I am the governor of my soul realm. I rule my emotions; they don't rule me. I choose the joy of the Lord as my dominant emotion.

James said that in order to count it all joy when you fall into a trial, you must know the divine purpose of trials—producing patience.[10] Your trial is a test—a test of your faith. Untested faith is of little value, but faith that has been tested and refined in the furnace of affliction is the most precious possession a person can have. It's more "precious than gold that perishes," and even though it is tested by fire, it "may be found to praise, honor, and glory at the revelation of Jesus Christ."[11]

We are not interested in a counterfeit faith that is nothing more than a naïve, humanistic optimism; we want fire-refined faith that has been proven in the tests of life. Four times in the Bible we are told to live by our faith.[12] The quality of your Christian life will be a reflection of the quality of your faith. Faith is the victory that overcomes the ubiquitous troubles we find in this world.[13] So, how do you know the quality of your faith? It is revealed in the tests of life—in the days of adversity. If we faint in adversity, our faith in God—the source of our strength—is small.[14]

On the night that Jesus was betrayed, He warned Peter that he was about to enter a great trial. Satan was out to get Peter![15] Satan had been observing Simon Peter, and he could not tell if Peter's faith was genuine or counterfeit. Satan, therefore, obtained permission from God to test Peter's faith. Notice that Satan had to ask God for permission before he could put Peter in a trial that would test his faith. The Bible promises that God will not allow you to be tested beyond what you can endure.[16] So, you can know for sure that you will never encounter a trial that is too great for your faith.

Jesus told Peter that he would be sifted as wheat. One of the ways wheat is sifted is to place it in a sieve and shake it violently; another way is to toss the grain in the air into a stiff breeze. I have seen this done in India many times. The purpose of this process is to separate the chaff from the wheat. Chaff is flaky stuff, but wheat has substance. When the wheat is thrown into the air, the wind carries the flaky chaff away, but the substantive grain falls back to the ground. This is what happens in a trial. You are tossed into the air in the midst of a strong wind, and the flaky stuff in your life is blown away, but your genuine faith will bring you back to the ground. Some people are all flaky stuff; they have no genuine faith in their lives. They may talk like they have faith and act like they have faith, but when the storm hits, all of their supposed faith turns out to be just flaky chaff that is blown away. After a while you cannot find these people; they are not in church anymore, they don't follow Jesus anymore, and they don't believe anymore. They never had real faith in the first place; they just had a flaky emotional experience that could not stand in the storm and failed the test of faith.

Jesus told Peter what would happen when he was tested, saying that Peter's faith would not fail.[17] Peter failed, but his *faith* did not completely fail. Peter failed in his courage, and he failed in his commitment, but his faith did not completely fail. There was a lot of flaky stuff in Peter that needed to be exposed and blown away. His boasting, his bravado, and his self-reliance were all flaky things that would be blown away in the trial. There was a genuine faith in Peter that enabled him to repent and return to Jesus. Like the wheat that is thrown into the air, the chaff is carried away, but the grain returns to the same place. This is the way it was with Peter. He was thrown into the air in the midst of a trial, and his pride was blown away, but his faith returned to Jesus.

The testing of our faith produces something—it produces patience.[18] The Greek word for *patience* used here is *hupomone*, which means, "cheerful consistency." When you have *hupomone* in the midst of your trial, you maintain the same cheerful attitude of victory. When you have *hupomone*, people may not be able to tell you are going through a trial, because you act the same way—you are cheerfully consistent. It is by exhibiting the patience of *hupomone* in the midst of a trial— admittedly a difficult spiritual skill to master—that you pass the test of your faith.

What happens if you don't pass the test? You don't fail, but you do get to take the test over. You will face this kind of test until you learn to pass the test by maintaining a cheerful and consistent attitude of victory no matter what your circumstances. This is *hupomone*. Sadly, it's a test the first generation of Israelites who came out of Egypt never did pass, and as a result, they were never able to enter the Promised Land, a land flowing with the milk of abundance and the honey of sweet victory. David, on the other hand, knew how to pass the faith test. Let's learn from David.

We all enjoy telling our own stories of God's deliverances, but without a test, there is no deliverance, no story, no testimony. Every glorious testimony that inspires the faith of others begins with a test. In the midst of a trial, the object is to turn the test into a testimony.

So, what happens when you add *hupomone* patience to fire-refined faith? James says you will lack nothing but will be "perfect and complete."[19]

It is God's will that you lack no good thing.[20] Though the devil's intent in the attack is to steal from you and diminish you, God will work with you in the midst of the trial to bring you into greater abundance. An amazing thing!

If we lack wisdom or any other thing that God has promised, all we need to do is "ask of God." He will never rebuke us for asking or refuse to respond. He "gives to all liberally," and we will lack nothing.[21]

Lack nothing—what a wonderful promise. If you can govern your emotions and maintain your joy, if you recognize your trial is nothing but a test of your faith, if you can maintain the cheerful consistency of patience, then in the end you will lack nothing. This is the promise of God!

Get a Word From God

DAVID WAS BEGINNING to recover from the initial shock of the tragedy brought about by the Amalekite raid on Ziklag. He had encouraged himself as he played his harp and praised God. His newfound courage had set him apart from the rest of the men, and once again they looked to him for leadership. As David reasserted his authority, the mutineers ceased their foolish talk of stoning him. Now every eye was upon their stalwart leader as they waited for his direction. What would he do?

David called for Abiathar. Abiathar was the only priest to escape the massacre of the priests by Saul and Doeg at Nob a few years earlier. Since that time, Abiathar had become a close personal friend of David and traveled with him in his journeys. He had been with David in Aphek and had returned with him to Ziklag.

When David wanted to fight a battle, he would call for Joab, but when David wanted to seek the Lord, he would call for Abiathar. David had never needed a word from God more desperately than he needed one now. He called for Abiathar.

When Abiathar came, David said to the priest, "Please bring me the ephod." The ephod was the garment of the priest. When David would seek the Lord, he would wear the linen ephod. When David brought the ark of the covenant into Jerusalem, he took off his kingly robes and wore the simple linen ephod of the priest—an act that deeply offended his status-conscious wife Michal (who was in every way a daughter of Saul).

As a type of Christ, David occupied all three offices of prophet, priest, and king. He composed psalms as a prophet, wore the ephod as a priest, and held the scepter as a king. For the New Testament believer, the prophetic, the priestly, and the kingly are all dimensions of life in Christ.

After Abiathar brought David the ephod, the men watched as David laid aside his weapons and armor and put on the simple linen ephod. Then David asked to be left alone. It was time for him to seek a word from God. Through the night David prayed...and waited...and listened. And then it came! It was what he needed most of all—the word of the Lord! It was unmistakable. It did not come to his head but to his heart. God does not speak to the mind but to the spirit. It was not a vague impression; it was a succinct sentence spoken by the Spirit of God into the deepest part of David's being: "Pursue, for you shall surely overtake them and without fail recover all."[1]

This was the word of the Lord for David. In the Hebrew it is only ten words. These ten words take only five seconds to speak. David may have sought the Lord for hours, but in five seconds, God gave David everything he needed to turn his tragedy into triumph. This is the power and potential of the Word of the Lord.

Hearing . . . and Hearing

When you are in trouble, what you need most of all is faith. It really is as simple as that. Faith is the victory. Faith is the victory that overcomes. But where does faith come from? The Bible tells us "faith comes by hearing, and hearing by the word of God."[2] Notice carefully what the Bible says. The Bible does not simply say that faith comes by hearing; it says "faith comes by hearing, and *hearing*." Hearing and hearing; there's a repetition to it, a repetitiveness about it. If you are going to develop overcoming faith, you can't just hear the Word. You need to hear the Word over and over again. You have to keep hearing and keep hearing the Word until it renews your mind, destroys doubt, and develops faith in your heart.

To understand how faith comes to a person, especially in times of great crisis, it is helpful to understand how the New Testament uses the word, *word*. When the New Testament says that faith comes by hearing, and hearing by the Word of God, it uses a particular Greek word for "word": *rhema*.

Rhema is different from another Greek word used for "word": *logos*. The difference between these two words can be subtle but is nevertheless significant. *Logos* is primarily word as an idea, a concept, a reason, a logic, and is very much related to that which is timeless. It is especially used to refer to the written word. *Logos* occurs in the Greek New Testament three hundred thirty times, and as such you might think of it as an ordinary word. *Rhema*, on the other hand, means a living, spoken word. It is more specific and more particular to time and place. It is the word for you in the moment. As such, *rhema* is less common in the Greek New Testament, occurring seventy times.

Consider this example. When Jesus invited Peter to come to Him by walking upon the sea, Jesus spoke a specific word to Peter in that time and place—Jesus said, "Come." The word *come* as it appears in the text of your Bible in a timeless way is a *logos* word.[3] Simply reading that Jesus said, "Come," to Peter will not generate faith in *you* to walk on water. (If you doubt this, I invite you to try it.) But in that specific moment when Jesus said, "Come," to Peter, for him it was a *rhema* word generating exceptional faith. In the time of crisis, exceptional faith is generated by the specific word God speaks to you. This is why David asked for the ephod—he needed to hear from God in the present moment.

Just as there are multiple Greek words for "word"—there are also multiple Greek words used in the New Testament for "time," specifically *chronos* and *kairos. Chronos* has to do with time on the move or the measurement of time. Thus, we have the word *chronological* (time is the measurement of movement through space). It is fair and accurate to think of *chronos* as ordinary time, but *kairos* is different. *Kairos* is a specific time or the right time or the now time. *Kairos* is always in the present. If *chronos* is ordinary time, *kairos* is special time. *Kairos* is the opportune moment.

Now let's put it all together. *Logos* corresponds with *chronos*, and *rhema* corresponds with *kairos*. Did you get that? There is a general word that is applicable at all times (*logos* and *chronos*). But there is a specific word that is applicable in a specific moment (*rhema* and *kairos*). When we read the story of Peter walking on the water with Jesus, it is a timeless story from which many general lessons can be derived. But when Jesus specifically says to *you*, "Come!" and you get out of the boat and walk on water, that is *rhema* meeting *kairos*! It's a specific word in a specific time. It is the *rhema* word in the *kairos* moment, which creates a miracle.

What David had received from the Lord as he wore the linen ephod was the *specific* word for the *specific* time—the *rhema* word in the *kairos* moment. That's what needs to happen following the worst day of your life. When you are in great trial, always remember this: God has a specific word for you in that situation. God has a *rhema* word for your *kairos* moment. Yes, it's the *rhema* word in the *kairos* moment that creates the miracle!

Thunder in Your Spirit

When seeking God for a word, be patient. Don't make up a word in your mind; seek God until you know He has spoken in your spirit. It may take some time. You can't always get a word from God in five minutes. But you will know it when God speaks. I have often described it as thunder in your spirit. As a pastor, I have seen a lot of people get in trouble because they thought they heard a word from God when all they have is a thought, a mere impression in their mind (probably based on their own desire).

God does not speak to your mind; God speaks to your spirit. God is not a "cosmic mind"; He is a Spirit.[4] When I talk about getting a word from God, I'm not talking about a vague impression. I'm talking about a specific word. It is not something you get every day. If you are going to discern the difference between thoughts in your mind and words from God, you have to know the difference between your soul (the realm of mind, will, and emotions) and the spirit (the part that is God-breathed and regenerated by the Holy Spirit). The way you learn this distinction is by constantly spending time in the Word of God. The soul and spirit are very closely related, even intertwined, and it is not always easy to tell the difference between the two. But the Word of God is like a surgeon's scalpel in the hands of the Holy Spirit, which can separate the two. God's Word is "living and powerful, and sharper than any two-edged sword."[5] It divides soul and spirit, joints and marrow, and it discerns the thoughts and intents of our hearts.

On your worst days, it's easy for your mind to run wild and for a thousand different thoughts to come crashing into your mind. This is not the word of the Lord. The *rhema* word of God in your *kairos* moment is something spoken to you by the Spirit of God in the deep recesses of your spirit. On my worst days, it has always been a specific word from God that has delivered me. Let me share three of my stories with you.

In June of 1977, I was eighteen years old. I had just graduated from high school and eagerly anticipated my future. I knew God had called me to the ministry, and I was anxious to get started. Two and half years earlier, I experienced a dramatic conversion and spent my remaining high school years being the resident "Jesus freak." Now that I had graduated high school, my plan was to attend a Bible college in California. And I was ready to go!

Then I became sick. I was sick enough to be on bedrest for two weeks. Though I often felt very sick, I spent most of that time reading the Bible. One night during those two weeks I felt like the Spirit of the Lord wanted me to change my plans and stay in Missouri. As I pondered this, God spoke to me very specifically: "You will build a great church in St. Joseph, Missouri, and travel the world preaching the gospel." Wow. That's pretty heady stuff for a long-haired Jesus freak from Savannah, Missouri—but I dared to believe it. I would stay in Missouri and eventually build a great church and travel the world preaching the gospel. Though I was still sick, that word made me very happy.

The next day, I received an extremely disturbing report from my doctor. I remember it as if it were yesterday. My family doctor, whom I had known all of my life, who delivered me into the world, who sat every Sunday on the third row of the Baptist church I attended, spoke these words: "We believe you have acute leukemia with six weeks to live." Most people never hear words quite so dramatic—a prognosis of six weeks to live when you're only eighteen. I can tell you those words got my attention.

But my reaction to those words was strange. I was more puzzled than shocked. It was a moment of cognitive dissonance. I was facing a deep incongruity. Things didn't line up. Last night I was certain God had spoken to me about building a great church in St. Joseph, Missouri, and about traveling the world preaching the gospel. And now a man I greatly respected was telling me I might very well be dead in six weeks. As funny as it sounds, I actually had a moment when I thought, "But I can't build a great church and travel the world in six weeks."

That night as I lay in my bed sick as ever and now quite discouraged, I thought, "I'd better read my Bible." That's also a bit funny considering I had been reading it day and night for two weeks. But I thought I might find some encouragement in the psalms, so I randomly chose Psalm 118 and began to read. I read the first sixteen verses rather mechanically, but when I got to the seventeenth verse, I froze when I read these words: "I shall not die, but live, and declare the works of the Lord."[6]

You can read those words all your life, and they may not mean much, but try reading them the day you receive a terminal diagnosis, and they will grab your attention. In that moment, *rhema* met *kairos*, and faith was born in my heart. I specifically remember taking my right index finger, tapping that verse in my New American Standard Bible, and saying out loud over and over, "I shall not die but live and declare the works of the Lord. I shall not die but live and declare the works of the Lord." This was not something I was accustomed to. At this point in my life, I didn't know anything about healing. I didn't even particularly believe in healing. I had never heard a sermon in my life on the subject of healing, but at that moment, I believed I would be healed. I simply had no doubt about it.

The next day my girlfriend, Peri, came to see me. I was eighteen, and I had a girlfriend! And I still have that girlfriend—she's been my wife for the past twenty-eight years! She had been told about the doctor's bad report, and when she came into my room, she was crying. When I saw her crying, there was something strangely funny about the moment, so I laughed and said, "I shall not die but live and declare the works of the Lord."

What happened? Well, I did not die. I have lived. I am still declaring the works of the Lord. There is a great church in St. Joseph, Missouri, and as I rewrite this chapter almost thirty-two years later, I'm in Rome, where I will be preaching the gospel on Sunday morning! It has all come to pass. Eventually the doctor concluded that his diagnosis must have been wrong because people with acute leukemia don't recover like I did. And of course, it was wrong. All I know is that when I read those words on that June night in 1977— "I shall not die, but live and declare the works of the Lord"—and when I spoke them aloud, something very powerful happened in me. I knew I would live and not die.

Four years later I founded Word of Life Church in St. Joseph, Missouri. I was twenty-two years old. Truth be told, I didn't know the first thing about founding or pastoring a church. I had great vision for the church, but that was about it. In those early years, things were very difficult. The church wasn't growing; we had few people and less money. Those who thought I was too young to be a pastor often criticized me. I probably was too young, but what was I to do? I was getting older as fast as I could. I was simply doing to the best of my ability what God had called me to do. But discouragement was a real enemy.

I remember one hot August afternoon after the church had been going (or not going!) for several years. I parked my red Toyota in front of our little red brick building we had purchased for sixty-five hundred dollars. As I looked at this decrepit old chapel, everything about it seemed to speak of failure—the broken sidewalk, the broken stained-glass windows, the broken steeple. Everything was broken. That's when a voice, quoting Scripture, spoke to my mind. The voice said, "You see that you are accomplishing nothing." I knew it was a Bible verse.[7] Since the voice quoted Scripture, I assumed it was God. I thought that God had decided I was a failure in the ministry and was telling me to get out. I walked into the building as the most dejected pastor in America. As I paced around in the tiny sanctuary I began to contemplate what else I might do. I finally decided to see if I could get a job at a menswear store selling suits. My reason for making this particular choice was that I didn't have any decent clothes and thought that in addition to making a living, perhaps this way I could get some clothes. Strange logic, I know. But I was honestly convinced I was supposed to leave the ministry because I was a failure.

As I headed for the door to go apply for a job at the menswear store, another voice, quoting another scripture, spoke to my mind. This voice said, "I would have lost heart, unless I had believed that I would see the goodness of the LORD in the land of the living."[8] Suddenly I realized the first voice that spoke to my mind was not God at all but a demon spirit trying to discourage me and get me to quit. And it almost worked. I almost quit. But now I had a real word from God—a *rhema* word in the *kairos* moment. And although no one was in the church building at the time, I ran on to the platform, got behind my pulpit, and preached a sermon from Psalm 27:13!

I shouted at the top of my lungs in that empty building and said, "I won't quit! I won't give up! I will see the goodness of God! Not when I die but right now! Here! In the land of the living!" Then I gave an altar call, jumped down off the platform, and responded to my own altar call, repenting of my doubt and unbelief! Yes, I really did this! A word from God kept me from quitting the ministry just as I was getting started.

By 1986, the church had grown some, but it was still small and a long way from my original vision. On April 1 of that year, I had gotten up early to go to my study. I stopped at Hardee's on the way to church and got a breakfast biscuit and a cup of coffee. I remember it all vividly. I went into my study, sat down at my secondhand, homemade desk purchased at an auction for thirty-five dollars, opened my Bible to Acts 16, and began to read. To this day I can tell you everything about that moment because a real experience with God will forever mark the time and place. I was planning to read five chapters, but that day I only read five verses. When I got to the fifth verse, I read these words: "So the churches were strengthened in faith, and increased in number daily."[9]

I was struck by those words "increased in number daily." They seemed to mock my frustration. I said out loud, between bites of my Hardee's biscuit, "Wouldn't that be nice?" In that moment, God spoke to me. It was totally unexpected. Although my mumbled complaint wasn't really a prayer, God chose to respond to it anyway. He spoke to me more clearly than at any other time in my life. God spoke seven words to me. It was not a vague impression; it was a sentence from the voice of God. It was not audible, but it was clearer than if it had been audible. It was like thunder in my spirit. God said to me, "Preach faith, and your church will grow."

Seven simple words. But those seven words from God totally changed my life and ministry. Those words were not a church growth strategy; they were a *rhema* word for me from God in my *kairos* moment! From that day on, everything changed in my ministry. Word of Life Church began to grow. Now there are several thousand people who call Word of Life their church home. I think about this event often. I certainly think about it every April 1. And I don't call it "April Fools' Day"; I call it "Faith Day."

Ten years after that event, I preached my first Sunday sermon in our brand-new, 2,500-seat auditorium. I titled the message "Ten Years of Faith." In ten years we had gone from a 120-seat chapel to a 2,500-seat auditorium, and it was all because of those seven words spoken by God.

These are my stories, but you need your own stories, and you can have them. God has a plan for you, and God has a word for you. When you're discouraged and ready to quit, God has a word for you. When you're afraid and about to panic, God has a word for you. When your world is falling and you don't know what to do, God has a word for you. When you are facing the worst day of your life and don't know where to turn, God has a word for you. Get alone with God. Wait in His presence. Listen for the still, small voice. In the *kairos* moment, God will give you a *rhema* word, and that's when miracles happen.

Reorient Your Vision

A S A NEW day began to dawn over Ziklag, a new day began to dawn in David's heart. He had spent the night wearing the linen ephod and seeking the Lord. In the middle of the night God had spoken to him and said, "Pursue, for you shall surely overtake them and without fail recover all." A day earlier everything seemed hopeless, but now things were changing. David had a word from God, and with that word David had found fresh faith and a new hope. Yesterday all David could see was a bleak future of loss and sorrow, but today he had a new vision—a vision of victory and recovering all. David had reoriented his vision from the dismal ashes of the present to the hopeful potential of the future.

As the men began to gather around David after their own sleepless night, they watched him take off the linen ephod and give it back to Abiathar. They could see that David looked different. He had that faraway look in his eyes; he could see something they could not see. David had the eye of the eagle. I can imagine one of David's chief lieutenants asking, "What is it, David? What do you see?"

I can hear David answering, "I see victory." Then David began to prophesy his vision to those men. "We are going to rise up. We are going to pursue the Amalekites who have destroyed our homes, stolen our possessions, and taken our families. We are going to overtake them, and without a doubt, we are going to recover all! Everything! Every wife, every son, every daughter. We are going to take back all of our livestock, all our silver, and all of our gold. We are going to recover all."[1]

Spontaneously the men began to shout and cheer. They held their swords high and shouted David's prophetic mantra, "Recover all!" Suddenly the negative energy of despondency and self-pity had been replaced by the positive energy of a new faith expectation. What had happened? A man of vision had prophesied hope back into hopeless men. He had reoriented their vision. Instead of focusing on what had happened and the loss of the present moment, these men now had a vision of recovery that energized them toward productive activity and a victorious future.

To recover all on the worst day of your life you must reorient your vision. The present crisis can cast you into darkness like a total eclipse of the sun. The crisis can move between you and the light of God, casting a dark shadow over your life and paralyzing you from engaging in productive activity. The terrible thing that has happened can appear so big that it seems impossible to focus on anything else. The crisis becomes the only thing you can see. That's when you must reorient your vision; you must find a way to look beyond the crisis and establish a vision of recovering all. That's when God's word is like a light shining in a dark place.

God's word to David was, "Pursue, for you shall surely overtake them and without fail recover all." David now knew that it was God's will for him to recover all. He was no longer hesitant. He was no longer beleaguered by doubt. Momentary doubt is the natural consequence of receiving the kind of blow that Ziklag delivers—it's like having the wind knocked out of you. It's having the faith knocked out of you. You must reorient your vision toward the promises of God in such a way that you recover your faith and shake off the doubt. He who doubts is like a wave upon the sea, driven and tossed by the wind. You will not receive anything from God while lingering in the duplicity of doubt. Doubt allowed to linger too long will produce dangerous emotional and spiritual instability.[2]

God Wants You to Recover

You must be convinced that God wants you to recover. You must be fully persuaded of God's unwavering love for you. You must know that God wants you to succeed in life. Faith begins where the will of God is known. How do you know the will of God? You study the Bible! Your Bible is a leather-bound copy of God's will for your life. Study it until you have no doubt about God's will for you. You cannot be wondering if God wants you to win or lose, succeed or fail, flourish or falter.

David said, "This I know . . . God is for me."[3] Let me help you with these four words: *God is for you!* Just as any good father wants his children to succeed in life, so your heavenly Father is for you. He wants you to succeed in life. Here are some promises from God for you to meditate on that will help you to reorient your vision. Better yet, memorize them. As you saturate your thinking in these promises, the eclipse of faith that has cast you into the darkness of doubt will pass away, and you will again find yourself walking in the cheerful sunshine of knowing God is for you.

> The LORD was with Joseph, and he was a successful man.[4]

> And the LORD will make you the head and not the tail; you shall be above only, and not be beneath, if you heed the commandments of the LORD your God, which I command you today, and are careful to observe them.[5]

> This Book of the Law shall not depart from your mouth, but you shall meditate in it day and night,

that you may observe to do according to all that is written in it. For then you will make your way prosperous, and then you will have good success.[6]

Let them shout for joy and be glad, who favor my righteous cause; and let them say continually, "Let the LORD be magnified, who has pleasure in the prosperity of His servant."[7]

The thief does not come except to steal, and to kill, and to destroy. I have come that they may have life, and that they may have it more abundantly.[8]

But thanks be to God, who gives us the victory through our Lord Jesus Christ.[9]

Now thanks be to God who always leads us in triumph in Christ.[10]

For people facing hard times, these precious promises are like "apples of gold in settings of silver."[11] They are diamonds from the Word of God that will help you reorient your vision. Instead of allowing the crisis to dictate a bleak outlook, the Word of God has the potential to produce within you an alternative imagination for the future. It's like the sun bursting through the clouds after days of gray and overcast skies.

Vision is all about your perspective on the future, and your perspective on the future determines whether you will be energized or demoralized. We live almost all of our lives in memory and imagination—remembering the past and imagining the future. We encounter the past by memory, and we encounter the future by imagination. The present is so brief as to be almost indefinable. *Now* is nothing more than the infinitesimal slice of time between memory and imagination. It is memory and imagination that allow us to hear melody. We remember the note we heard a second ago and imagine the anticipated note, and thus we encounter melody. Without memory and imagination there would be no melody in our lives, just a stupefying preoccupation with the present moment. But when malevolent forces are allowed to dominate our memory and imagination, we can suffer severe mental torment. It's hell inside your head, and this is intolerable. In order to be happy, humans need healed memories and hopeful imaginations. God's Word is capable of accomplishing both of these tasks.

The truth that we live most of our lives in memory and imagination is undeniable. We remember the past and imagine the future. Our past is fixed (though our perspective on the past can change—more about that later), but the future is unknown. The only way we can relate to the future is through imagination. Imagination is indeed a legitimate way of knowing. Hope is the God way of imagining the future. A mind that is God-conscious, God-centric, and God-saturated will be full of hope. It's hope that energizes us for positive action.

Don't allow the malignant cancer of worry to dominate your imagination. Both worry and hope deal with an unknown future, and you have every right to imagine a bright future created by hope. This is what David was doing. Instead of allowing worry and anxiety to dictate his future, David, through a reoriented vision of victory, was imagining a future framed by hope. This hopeful imagination energized both David and his men to begin to engage in positive action—positive action that had the potential to change their situation.

Get a Vision of Victory

Human beings are mysterious creatures who are powerfully affected by vision. We are designed in such a way that we will move in the direction of what we see. Your vision is your future, and your vision is your imagination. You need an imagination inspired by the promises of God, and you need to develop a vision of victory. You need the eye of the eagle. The eagle builds its nest high atop a mountain or tall rock. From there, "it spies out the prey; its eyes observe from afar."[12]

Do you have the eye of the eagle? Can you see from afar? Can you see into the distant horizon of your future to view the glorious things that God has prepared for you? God has not called you to be a chicken pecking around in the barnyard of the status quo, never seeing anything but the dust of Old McDonald's farm. God has called you to mount up on the eagle's wings of faith and soar above the storms.[13] God has given new creation man the eye of the eagle to behold destiny at a great distance.

I have found that I remain excited about life as long as I hold on to the vision that hope can create. As I live in the realm of hopeful vision, I find I can begin each new day with fresh energy and enthusiasm. This is the power of vision. Vision is not simply your wants, wishes, and desires—vision is what you see! Vision is the image of the future that dominates your imagination. If you ask a man living an empty, dead-end life if he wishes he had a better life, he would certainly say yes. But he has no vision for it. He wishes things were better, but as he peers into his future, all he sees is more of the same. He's like Bill Murray in the movie *Groundhog Day*, living the same day over and over. Your vision is not merely your wants, wishes, and desires—your vision is what you see. Your vision is your future!

Georgian Banov is a close friend of mine, and like many of my friends, he is a musician. Georgian plays guitar and piano and is a classically trained violinist. He grew up in Bulgaria in the 1960s when the communist officials kept a tight rein on music and the arts. One day Georgian heard the Beatles on Radio Free Europe singing, "I Want to Hold Your Hand." It was a moment that changed Georgian's life. Soon Georgian formed a rock band, and they began to play throughout Bulgaria. They were an instant sensation, that is until the state police deemed their music as a capitalistic excess that would corrupt the young people of Bulgaria and pulled the plug on them in the middle of a concert.

That's when Georgian decided it was time to get out of Bulgaria, or, as Georgian says, "When the state stops your music, it's time to get a new state." He found a way into East Germany, and from there was able to escape to the political freedom of West Germany. Eventually, Georgian wound up in California during the height of the Jesus Movement. He was introduced to the gospel, became a Christian, and formed the band Silverwind.

In the early days of our church when we were still quite small, I invited Georgian to minister on a Friday night. Before the service, we were talking in my study, and he asked me about my vision. As I began to share my vision, a passion rose up in me, and the words poured forth. It seemed like a holy moment. Suddenly, Georgian jumped up, came over to where I was sitting, began poking me in the chest with his finger, and said these words to me: "Keep your mind on your vision. Make a decision! Keep your mind on your vision. Make a provision! Keep your mind on your vision. Tell all distractions good-bye."

I have never forgotten those words. They have often been a help to me. Even now I think about them often. Keep your mind on your vision! This is what David had to do. God's prophetic word had reoriented his vision, and now David had to make a decision, a provision. He had to keep his mind on his vision and tell all distractions good-bye. If you are going to move your life beyond catastrophe and in the direction of recovery, you have to reorient your vision toward victory, and then keep your mind locked in on that vision.

Increase Your Capacity for Vision

As I read the scriptural account of the Old Testament prophets, it seems as though God is very interested in a person's capacity for vision. Repeatedly in Scripture God asks people this question: "What do you see?" "What do you see, Jeremiah?" "What do you see, Zechariah?" "What do you see, Ezekiel?" "What do you see, Amos?" It's the question God presents to prospective prophets. To be a prophetic person who has some sense of what God is doing, you need a certain capacity for vision.

How do you improve your spiritual vision? By saturating your mind in Scripture. This enhances your capacity for vision. Disciplined reading of Scripture is an exercise in reading God's thoughts after Him, and it expands your capacity to think the God thoughts necessary to transcend convention and move beyond present limitation. You will never go further than your vision, and if you have moles' eyes instead of eagles' eyes you will be very limited. To move beyond the ashes of your worst day you need a new vision. If you can see the invisible, you can do the impossible.

In my life and ministry there have been times when I attempted new things that seemed risky at the time. But I had seen something, and I was going to be daring enough to move in the new direction of a new vision. This doesn't mean that everything I have attempted has been successful, but one thing is certain: without a new vision, you will never have anything new. You will be perpetually stuck in the vicious cycle of the religion of the wheel. This is what makes life seem like an exercise in futility, and this frustrating absurdity is what is depicted so poetically in the Book of Ecclesiastes:

> "Everything is meaningless," says the Teacher, "completely meaningless!" What do people get for all their hard work under the sun? Generations come and generations go, but the earth never changes. The sun rises and the sun sets, then hurries around to rise again. The wind blows south, and then turns north. Around and around it goes, blowing in circles. Rivers run into the sea, but the sea is never full. Then the water returns again to the rivers and flows out again to the sea. Everything is wearisome beyond description. No matter how much we see, we are never satisfied. No matter how much we hear, we are not content. History merely repeats itself. It has all been done before. Nothing under the sun is truly new.[14]

Many people misunderstand the purpose of the Book of Ecclesiastes. Ecclesiastes is a revelation of a life lived without a personal relationship with God. The personal name of God, *Jehovah*, never appears in the Book of Ecclesiastes. Ecclesiastes is a depressing book, not one to turn to when you need encouragement and need to have your faith built. The recurrent phrase, "under the sun," is euphemistic of the idea that there is no God in heaven. It is a description of the futility of life without a vibrant connection with the living God.

Ecclesiastes describes the religion and philosophy of the wheel. Life goes in circles, but nothing ever changes. Everything is vanity. Everything is absurdity. What has been is what will be. What has been done is what will be done. There is nothing new under the sun. It's the idea that life is ultimately an inescapable cycle, a vicious circle. It's the philosophy that dominates Eastern religion and Eastern philosophical thought. It is the system of religion and thought out of which God called Abraham.

Abraham originally lived in the Sumerian civilization of Mesopotamia (modern-day Iraq) in the cosmopolitan city of Ur. The Sumerians of ancient Mesopotamia were no backwater primitives. They built one of the first advanced civilizations. They were the first to utilize a written language and advanced mathematics. Ur in particular was a city of culture and sophistication. I've seen the ancient art of Ur in the British Museum, and it leaves you with the distinct impression that these were a highly cultured people. The city of Ur had the largest library in the ancient world, an advanced sewer system, and considerable understanding of medicine and mathematics. But despite the intellectual and technical sophistication of Ur, God called Abraham out of Ur as He began to form His alternative society. Why?

The primary deity worshiped by the Sumerians was Nanna-Sin, the moon god. Nanna-Sin was the god of the cycles (as in the lunar cycle). At the heart of the worship of Nanna-Sin was the philosophy of the wheel, the fatalistic notion that we all live in an inescapable circle. It is a philosophy that says what has been is what will be, what has been done is what will be done, and there is nothing new under the sun.

But God called Abraham to break out of the vicious circle and journey to a new place. (What a wonderful word *journey* is!) In order for Abraham to embark upon a journey into the unknown—for him to leave behind everything he knew to go wherever his faith in God led him—required a tremendous ability for vision. Abraham would have to believe there really could be something new under the sun.

Abraham would eventually become eternally famous for his faith and be known around the world as the *father of faith*. But Abraham's first step of faith was to turn his back on Ur and move toward something new, new but unknown. As Abraham left Ur, the last thing he would have seen would have been the ziggurat of the Nanna-Sin temple towering over Ur. Abraham had turned his back on the demon of the vicious circle. Abraham had a vision of something new and was breaking free from the religion and philosophy of the wheel.

If you are going to break from the vicious circle of addiction, depression, family strife, generational poverty, spiritual emptiness, and dead-end living, you must first reorient your vision toward something new and better.

Everyone wants good things—a good home and a good family, a good and happy marriage, and a good and meaningful life. But where do these good things come from? Are they simply inherited? Do we just hope we get lucky and somehow end up with good things? Where do good things come from? Jesus gave us the answer when He said that a good man brings forth good things "out of the good treasure of his heart," but an evil man brings forth evil things "out of the evil treasure" of his heart.[15]

The good things in a good man's life come from within him. They begin as part of his vision. They are first born in a hopeful imagination. I meet with pastors frequently who want to know how they can build a good church. I always tell them a good church begins in the heart of the pastor. A church will never be better than the pastor's vision. Are you longing for some good things in your life? You must first develop the vision inside of you. Of course, there is more to having good things in your life than just vision, but vision is the place where you start. David was a great leader because he had the essential quality of true leadership—he was able to communicate a new vision to his followers. David's men were ready to stone him until he was able to communicate to them his reoriented vision of recovering all.

When you have been through the worst day of your life, you need to reorient your vision and imagination. You need to turn your focus away from the present crisis and toward the alternative future of recovery. This is what hope is all about. See yourself transcending your tragedy, even if you're not sure yet how to get there. See yourself recovering all, even if it seems impossible right now. See yourself coming out of your present trouble into a place of genuine victory.

Let hope paint a new picture on the canvas of your imagination. Your vision will give you the courage to face tomorrow with new energy and strengthened resolve. With something as simple as a hope-oriented vision, you are on the road to recovering all.

Regain Your Passion

B Y THE TIME David had finished proclaiming his reoriented vision of total victory and recovering all, the sun was climbing high over the eastern horizon. The men had been inspired by David's prophetic declaration of "pursue and recover all," and they were ready to fight. There was a tangible excitement in the air. David said, "Strap on your weapons; we're going after the Amalekites!" David was able to find out from the few who had escaped the Amalekite attack that after leaving Ziklag, the Amalekites headed south. So David and the six hundred men with him marched south.

Under the searing Judean sun, they marched all morning and into the afternoon until they reached the Brook Besor.

The exhausted men eagerly waded into the cool brook to quench their thirst and refresh their tired bodies. After a short rest, David said, "It's time to go; we've got to catch up with the Amalekites." But many of the men were just too exhausted to go any farther. They had been marching for four days, from Aphek to Besor, and many of them had reached the limit of their strength. It was decided that two hundred of the men would stay at Besor and watch over the supplies while the other four hundred continued the pursuit of the Amalekites.

Not long after David and the four hundred pursuers left Besor, they got the break they needed. After crossing the brook, they found an Egyptian slave lying semiconscious in an open field. He had been left for dead by his Amalekite master after he had fallen sick three days earlier. They gave the half-dead Egyptian some water, fed him some figs and raisin muffins, and in a short while, the man revived. David struck a deal with the Egyptian, promising to spare him his life and not to turn him over to the Amalekites if he would lead them to the enemy camp. The Egyptian readily agreed, and now David was closing in on the men who had committed the grievous crimes against him.

As the sun was setting, the Egyptian told David they were near. He took David to the top of a ridge, and down below were the Amalekites. David hid behind the rocks and crept closer. There they were—thousands of Amalekites spread out over the valley floor. They were eating and drinking and dancing.

As David watched from his hiding place, his blood began to boil in anger. The Amalekites were feasting on his lambs! They were drinking his wine out of his cups! Bags full of his gold and silver were slung across the backs of camels. And they were dancing! Dancing because they had enriched themselves at David's expense.[1] There were David's wives, Ahinoam and Abigail, being forced to dance with drunken Amalekites. David's children sat huddled together, eyes wide with terror. David's mind was now blind with rage! The Amalekites didn't know it yet, but they had made a very big mistake. David was mad...really, really mad.

On the worst day of your life, there is a time to weep, but there is also a time to get mad. There is a time to shake off passivity and resignation and regain your passion. If you want to direct your anger toward a personality, then get mad at the devil. Earlier, David's men had been angry with David— angry enough to speak of stoning him. But David was not their problem or their enemy. Be careful about directing your anger in the wrong direction. Regaining passion is a necessary aspect of placing yourself in a position of recovering all, but don't misdirect your anger toward the wrong people—better yet, don't direct your anger toward people at all. In his letter to the Ephesians, the apostle Paul gives an important insight into the spiritual nature that underlies all reality by stating that our conflict is ultimately not with human beings but with demonic personalities in the spiritual realm.[2]

Passion Is Required for Action

Passion is a necessary emotion for action. If you are going to have sufficient energy to embark upon recovering all, you need to regain your passion. Anger is an appropriate passion when directed toward evil and the ultimate source of evil. Even hatred is a necessary corollary of love. Because God loves humanity, He hates sin and Satan. When understood properly, it is appropriate, even necessary, for us to share in God's hatred of evil. When David spoke concerning the enemies of God, he called them his enemies also and said, "I hate them with perfect hatred."[3]

Of course, in the light of what we understand from the New Testament, it should be clear that hatred is *never* to be directed toward other human beings, even those who are undeniably our enemies. Jesus clearly taught us to love our enemies. This is nonnegotiable. But Jesus's mandate to love our enemies does not apply to the world of absolute irredeemable evil in the spiritual realm over which Satan rules. Simply put, you don't have to love the devil. Jesus never had anything but a contemptuous attitude toward demons, and He was passionate in His contempt.

When we consider the works of the devil, it should make us angry. When we think about the evils of war, violence, injustice, poverty, disease, human trafficking, child abuse, and the awful toll such evils exact upon human lives, it should make us angry indeed. A dispassionate attitude toward crimes like genocide, racism, or torture is unacceptable. To remain unmoved by these injustices is both inhuman and inhumane.

God has an intense anger toward evil. In part, hell can be understood as God's eternal wrath toward irredeemable evil. This is why hell was created. Hell is not God's intention for human beings. Jesus speaks of hell being created for the devil and his angels.[4] Nevertheless, humans can give themselves so completely over to wickedness that there is no place left for them but the hell created for the devil and his angels. The final mention of the devil in the Bible reveals God's eternal attitude toward personified evil. In one final display of His hatred of the devil and his evil angels, Jesus cast them into the lake of fire, where "they will be tormented day and night forever and ever."[5]

The mission of Messiah was a kind of "seek and destroy" mission. He came to seek and save the lost and to destroy the works of the devil. When it comes to spiritual warfare, Jesus was no pacifist. Jesus waged a spiritual war on the devil and his demons. The apostle John described Jesus's mission by saying He came "that He might destroy the works of the devil."[6]

Jesus was frequently angry but never sinned in His anger. Paul reminds us to "be angry, and do not sin."[7] Jesus's anger was never based in selfishness or personal offense. Jesus was angry with sin, angry with hypocrisy, angry with religious abuse, and Jesus was always angry at the devil and his works. When Jesus encountered those who were demonically tormented, He experienced a mixture of emotions. Jesus felt compassion for the suffering person but immense anger toward the tormenting spirit. It was this kind of passion and compassion that fueled the ministry of Jesus.

Jesus enjoyed a close personal friendship with Lazarus and his two sisters, Mary and Martha.[8] Their home was in Bethany, just a few miles from Jerusalem, and it seems that Jesus was frequently their guest when He traveled to Jerusalem for the Jewish feasts. So, when Lazarus fell gravely ill, Mary and Martha sent word to Jesus in Galilee, but by the time Jesus reached Bethany, Lazarus had already been dead for four days.

As we read John's account, it is quite apparent that the scene was one of heart-wrenching sorrow. Lazarus's death was untimely, and it left his two sisters devastated. Both Mary and Martha expressed thinly veiled anger at Jesus for His delay in coming to Bethany, and both women were clearly distraught.

When Jesus was taken to the tomb and witnessed the inconsolable sorrow of the family and friends, it was too much. "Jesus wept."[9] Jesus wept because He had lost a friend. Jesus wept because He was human, and He too felt the sting of loss. Jesus wept because He was a man of compassion and was surrounded by heartbroken people. Perhaps Jesus also wept because He understood that death is unavoidable and every friendship ends in a funeral. Perhaps Jesus wept because the grave has been the bane of human existence since Adam and Eve buried their son Abel. Jesus wept at this grave for all the same reasons that you and I weep at graves and perhaps also for reasons that are beyond our comprehension. Yes, Jesus was overcome with sorrow and compassion to the point that it moved Him to tears, but this is not the only emotion Jesus experienced at the tomb of Lazarus.

Out of Jesus's compassion there rose a passion. From the sorrow that Jesus shared with the loved ones of Lazarus arose an anger at death itself. As Jesus stood there with His grief-stricken friends, He "groaned."[10] When He stood before the tomb of his friend, He was "groaning in Himself."[11]

The word translated "groan" is probably not the best translation of *embrimaomai*. This word is better understood as "growling" or "snorting" with anger. Eugene Peterson in *The Message* has translated this word as "deep anger." *Embrimaomai* is not a word associated with the emotion of sorrow but with the emotion of anger. Jesus felt the emotion of sorrow when He wept, but when He "groaned" or "growled" (*embrimaomai*), He felt the emotion of anger. Jesus felt compassion toward the grieving friends and family, but toward death Jesus felt the passion of anger. At the tomb of Lazarus, Jesus not only wept in sorrow, but He also growled in anger. Jesus then moved into action. He commanded the stone to be rolled back and then shouted with a loud voice, "Lazarus, come forth!"[12]

On that day, Jesus raised one man from the dead (it was really a temporary resuscitation, for Lazarus, of course, would die again). But there is a day coming when the Son of God will shout again and the redeemed will come forth from their graves never to die again![13]

It was the empathy of compassion alone that moved Jesus to raise Lazarus from the dead, and there was an element of holy anger involved. Passivity and acquiescence are no way to go about changing your life. If you want to change your life or circumstances in a profound way, passion is required. Has the devil hindered you, harassed you, or afflicted you? Get mad about it. Is it evident that Satan is influencing your children and leading them away from God? Get mad about it. Have the powers of darkness been behind destructive and negative events in your life? Get mad about it! Regain your passion! Get fighting mad! You won't be able to fight your way to victory unless you feel some anger over what the devil has done.

As a kid, my nickname was Fry. I got it in the fourth grade because of my temper. I would get so mad that I would just fry, so that is what my friends called me! As a consequence of my temper, I got in plenty of fights. One fight in particular stands out in my memory. It happened in the seventh grade. I was on the basketball team, and one day during practice another player and I got into a shoving match on the court. The coach pulled us apart, but the other boy said, "I'll see you after practice, Fry!" Of course, that meant we were going to fight, and I had a problem—this boy was much bigger than I was!

Once my temper cooled, I had no interest in fighting him. So, after practice I took my time showering and changing, hoping he would forget about it. He didn't. When I walked out of the locker room, he was waiting for me. Of course, nothing draws a crowd in seventh grade like news of a fight, so everybody was there to see the fight. Because I was afraid of him I didn't put up much of a fight. He hit me a few times, knocked me to the ground, and that was it. The big kid was walking away, and I was lying on the ground. But as I heard some of the bystanders laughing, I got mad. I decided that being laughed at was worse than getting beat up. Then I got real mad. So I jumped up, ran after him, jumped on his back, pulled his stocking cap down over his head (it was winter), and proceeded to knock the daylights out of him.

Some of you have just been beat up by the devil. You've been afraid, you've been hit hard, you've been knocked down, and it's been painful. But now it's time to get mad. Don't just lie there and let the devil laugh at you. Get mad, get up, and begin to fight. I'll tell you a secret: The devil is counting on you not getting back up, because if you do, it changes everything. Satan is hoping you will stay passive, because passivity is not an attribute of the victorious Christian life.

A central concept in Eastern philosophy is liberation from suffering through the extinguishing of desire. This concept is known as *nirvana*. The word *nirvana* means "to blow out" or "extinguish." According to the philosophy of *nirvana*, the way to deal with suffering is to extinguish all desire. The Bible teaches us that we can overcome evil desires, such as lust, greed, and prideful ambition, but the Eastern philosophy of *nirvana* teaches its followers to do away with desire. This is contrary to being a real human! Desire is the drive of life!

Christian teaching differs from the Eastern philosophy in

that the Bible does not at all condemn desire itself. Desire is an essential part of being human and is a necessary element for human advancement. While it's true that desire can be corrupted into sinful forms of lust, greed, and ambition, desire itself remains part of what it means to be created in the image of God. The attempt to rid ourselves of all desire is ultimately self-destructive.

Discover the Value of Desire

God's Word teaches us the value of desire. God promises to respond to us "according to your heart's *desire*, and fulfill all your purpose."[14] We are to delight in the Lord, and if we do, He will "give you the *desires* of your heart."[15] God promises to reward our great faith by responding "as you *desire*."[16]

The promise is that if we express our desires to God when we pray and believe that God is going to grant those desires, "you will have them."[17] God says, "If you abide in Me, and My words abide in you, you will ask what you *desire*, and it shall be done for you."[18]

Desire really is the drive of life. If you are going to move toward full recovery, you need to regain a passionate desire to live in such a way as to be fully alive. As the church father Irenaeus said, "The glory of God is a man fully alive."

Satan would love for you to remain passive and docile. Demons spirits would be delighted if you would simply lose your fight, lie down, and give up. In fact, the depressive urge to lie down and quit is very often demonic in origin. The prophet Isaiah depicts a defeated people who have lost all capacity to fight and have passively become doormats for their tormentors. He says that our tormenters will taunt us, saying, "Lie down, that we may walk over you." Isaiah then says that we have actually responded to those taunts and "have laid your body like the ground...for those who walk over."[19]

Notice what the tormentors say: "Lie down that we may walk over you." Is that what you are going to do? Are you just going to lie down and be the devil's doormat? Are you going to allow demon spirits to tread upon you, when the Word of God says that it is your destiny to tread upon them?[20] If you are ever going to break the cycle of oppression and failure, you are going to have to get mad! The devil is never going to feel sorry for you. He is never going to feel pity for you. He is merciless, malevolent, and doesn't know the meaning of remorse. If you are going to shake off demonic oppression, you are going to have to regain your passion.

When David saw the Amalekites dancing, it totally engaged his passion. He was ready to fight. Don't let the devil dance over your defeat. The game isn't over. You're not out. If you'll regain your passion and renew the fight, things can change dramatically in your situation.

Attack!

HEN DAVID RETURNED from scouting out the Amalekite camp that the Egyptian slave had led them to, he gathered his men and gave them his report. He told them the Amalekite camp was just over the next ridge. He related to them what he had seen—he had seen their stolen possessions, their flocks and herds, their silver and gold. He told them how the Amalekites were feasting and dancing over the loot they had stolen from Ziklag. Most importantly, though, David told them he had seen their wives and children. They were being held captive by the Amalekites. The Amalekites were probably on their way to Egypt to sell them as slaves. The very idea of their wives and children in chains and being sold in the slave markets of Egypt was no doubt a bitter pill.

David met with Joab, Abishai, Shammah, and some of his other captains to plan their strategy of attack. It was now or never. They decided to attack at sundown. It was true that they were badly outnumbered, at least five to one, maybe more, but that didn't matter. They were fighting for their families, and each one would fight with the strength of ten men. Besides, they knew they had the God of Abraham, Isaac, and Jacob on their side. They believed that the God who had fought with Joshua at Jericho would fight with them now.

As the sun set, David's four hundred men silently crept to the top of the ridge. There they were—the Amalekites were feasting and dancing, celebrating the loot they had carted off from Ziklag. Cowering in fear in the nearby shadows were their families—what David and his men were really fighting for. Did they offer a quick prayer? Knowing David, I suspect so. Then David gave the command: attack![1] The men swooped down upon the unsuspecting Amalekites in their drunken revelry. An Amalekite watchman sounded the alarm, but it was too late. The enraged Israelites were already upon them. David and his men swung their swords with a ferocity they had never known before. They had fought for their lives many times, but never had they fought for their wives and children.

David and his men took no prisoners in this battle. They gave no quarter to the marauders. Fifteen years earlier at the battle of Shur, King Saul had spared Agag, the king of the

Amalekites. It was this failure to fully carry out the command of the Lord that had set in motion the events that would eventually lead to King Saul's downfall. David wouldn't make that mistake. The only ones able to escape the surprise attack were some of the younger and faster Amalekites who sped away on camels—about four hundred of them. The battle raged through the night and throughout the next day, from sundown to sundown. With almost supernatural endurance, David and his men avenged themselves on the Amalekites until they recovered their families and possessions. As the sun was setting after twenty-four hours of fighting, the battle was at last over. David and his men had faced their enemies, attacked them with the courage that comes from love of hearth and home, and they had prevailed. They had won the battle of their lives.

The Old Testament war stories of David and Joshua and the other Israelite warriors provide us with a powerful metaphor to help us understand how deadly serious our struggle is with the principalities and powers of darkness, these wicked spirit beings who are intent on ruling the world and ruining lives. This struggle is real. We can't wish it away. We can't just blithely wish for a nice, quiet life and hope that fate will treat us kindly. Like it or not, we are engaged in a deadly struggle with spiritual wickedness. As Martin Luther observed, this is a world with "devils filled."* Once you have identified the

---

* "A Mighty Fortress Is Our God" by Martin Luther. Public domain.

work of the devil in your life, you need to adopt an aggressive fighting attitude and attack it.

Use Your Arsenal of Divine Weapons

The powers of darkness that Paul describes in his epistles and that Jesus regularly encountered in the Gospels are like the Amalekites who waited for an opportune moment to attack Ziklag and steal every good thing. The apostle Peter describes Satan as a roaring lion, prowling about, seeking human lives to devour. The satanic intention is destructive and murderous. The thief comes to steal, kill, and destroy. The demonic aim is to take away every good thing God has given and everything good God intends for your life. If you are going to counter these attacks and recover what has been lost, you have to adopt an aggressive posture, press the battle, and attack. Since our struggle is not against flesh and blood but against spiritual entities, the New Testament speaks in terms of the spiritual weapons we have at our disposal—weapons that are spiritually sophisticated and highly effective in our struggle against spiritual wickedness.[2]

These weapons contain the power of God and are capable of giving you victory in your battles with the powers of darkness. To refer back to David, his battle with the Amalekites was not David's first fight with Gentile invaders. When David confronted Goliath in the Valley of Elah as a teenager fifteen years earlier, he did so with an unusual choice of weapon—a sling and five smooth stones in his shepherd's pouch. As a Christian, you have at least "five smooth stones," five highly effective weapons you can use against the Goliaths of our age. Let's briefly examine this arsenal of divine weapons.

The Word of God. The Word of God is called the sword of the Spirit.[3] In the Book of Revelation, the glorified Christ is described as having a sword that proceeds from His mouth.[4] Jesus wins His battle, not with the carnal sword of military armament, but with the spiritual sword of the Word of God. The Word of God becomes a sword of the Spirit when it has been hidden in your heart and spoken with your mouth. It's the Word of God in your heart and in your mouth that is a sword. Jesus prevailed in His battle with satanic temptation in the wilderness by using the Word of God and saying three times, "It is written."[5]

The Word of God is such a potent weapon against Satan's schemes because Satan's primary tactic has always been to lie. Lying is what the devil does. Jesus called Satan a liar and the father of lies. The way we overcome the lies of the devil is not through the capacity of human reason but through boldly speaking the Word of God. To be able to do this effectively, you need to spend time memorizing Scripture. In this way, you will be prepared in the hour of attack to deftly handle the sword of the Spirit. Like Jesus in His wilderness battle, you will be able to confidently say, "It is written!" This is the sword of the Spirit in use, and you need a *sword* of the Spirit, not a *pocketknife* of the Spirit. Knowing John 3:16 and "Jesus wept" is not enough. You need a real sword. Like Ehud, the Old Testament deliverer and judge, you must build your own sword.[6] You do this in quiet hours spent in Scripture meditation and memorization.

The name of Jesus. The name of Jesus is the authoritative name of the kingdom of God. Because of His act of obedience to the Father in going to the Cross, Jesus has been exalted and given the name above every name. We are told that every knee in three worlds—heaven, earth, and hell—must bow to the authority of Jesus's name.[7] As we engage the powers of darkness in battle, we don't do so in our own name or authority. We do so in the name of the Son of God, who has been given authority to subject all things to Himself.[8] The name of Jesus is the authority to cast out demons. The name of Jesus is the authority to heal the sick. The name of Jesus is the authority to bind and loose. The name of Jesus is the authority to forgive sins. The name of Jesus is the authority to destroy the works of the devil. Faith in the name of Jesus is the assertion that Jesus really is King of kings and Lord of lords—or, as we would think of it, President of presidents and Prime Minister of prime ministers. (Admittedly, this doesn't roll off the tongue as easily, but it helps capture the true nature of the authority that is contained in the name of Jesus.) All authority in heaven and earth is contained in the name of Jesus.

The blood of Jesus. The blood of Jesus is a weapon that causes every demon to flee in terror. It is the weapon that will silence the accuser of the brethren. The overcoming saints depicted in the Book of Revelation are those who know how to overcome the devil by the blood of the Lamb and the word of their testimony.[9] When you base your cause not on your own merits but on the blood of Jesus, and testify of that blood, it releases the power of God to overcome in your life.

Blood is mysterious. Leviticus speaks of blood being sacred because the essence of life is in the blood.[10] In a mysterious way, blood has a voice. God heard the voice of Abel's blood crying out from the ground.[11] The assertion that redemption is in the blood is central to the gospel. All ancient cultures understood that a blood sacrifice is essential for the remission of sins.[12] Life, voice, redemption—they all belong to blood. The life of Jesus that gives us eternal life is found in the blood of Jesus. The voice of Jesus that cries out for mercy and blessing is found in the blood of Jesus. The forgiveness of sins that sets us free is found in the blood of Jesus. In your struggle against Satan as the accuser, no weapon is more powerful than the blood of Jesus.

Prayer and praise. Prayer and praise are a kind of double-barrel shotgun. They both have to do with our direct engagement with God in worship. There is a multitude of stories in the Bible that serve the purpose of teaching us that prayer is the direct path to spiritual power. Abraham was a man of prayer and became the father of faith. Moses was a man of prayer and led a nation out of bondage. Joshua was a man of prayer, and the sun stood still. David was a man of prayer and was Israel's greatest warrior. Elijah was a man of prayer and worked great miracles. Isaiah was a man of prayer and saved Israel from foreign invasion. Daniel was a man of prayer and was spared in the lion's den. And Jesus was a man of prayer.

The Gospel of Luke in particular emphasizes the prayer life of Jesus. Before every major event in His life, we find Jesus stealing away to the secret place of prayer. Before facing temptation, before beginning His ministry, before choosing His disciples, before His great healing campaigns, before His transfiguration, before going to the Cross, we find Jesus in prayer. Jesus understood the connection between prayer and power. Jesus even explained to His disciples that some demons could not be cast out except by much prayer.[13] On the worst day of your life, if you are going to win the battle against the demonic onslaught, you must give yourself to prayer.

Praise is the other barrel of prayer. When you praise God, there is a powerful force in the spirit realm released against Satan and demons. Satan cannot function well in the atmosphere that is saturated with the high praises of God. It seems as though praise creates confusion among the enemies of God. This is clearly seen in the story of King Jehoshaphat's victory over the Ammonites and Moabites.[14] Jehoshaphat sent the singers of Israel before the army, and God responded to their praise by fighting the battle for them. Praise will also set you free from demonic bondage in the midnight hours of your life. We see this in the miraculous story of the deliverance of Paul and Silas from the Philippian jail. When they sang the praises of God, though in chains in the jail's dungeon, God responded by sending an earthquake and setting them free—and saving the jailer in the process.[15] I know it's hard, but if you can praise God on the worst day of your life—not because you feel like it, but because, no matter what, God is worthy of praise—it is a powerful form of spiritual warfare.

The Cross. Ultimately, all spiritual victory flows from the victory God won at the Cross of Christ. Yes, the Cross is the victory of God! The Cross of Christ is not just a historical event; it is also a perpetual spiritual reality. The Cross is an everlasting fountain of spiritual power. The Cross is the single greatest demonstration of the wisdom and power of God. Paul describes it as the deep wisdom that none of the principalities and powers understood. If they had understood the deep wisdom of God in the power of the Cross, they would never have crucified the Lord of glory.[16] The Cross is the great and holy mystery of God, which confounded the rulers of this age. Here the Son of God was cursed and hung on a tree, here the Son of God suffered the humiliation and agony of crucifixion, here the Son of God was put to death by a conspiracy of the imperial powers, and here God won His greatest victory. At the Cross God triumphed over sin, Satan, death, hell, and the grave! At the Cross:

- The debt of sin was paid in full.
- Humanity was elevated from the fall.
- Satan's dominion came to an end.
- The curse of the law was canceled.
- Alienation became reconciliation.
- Hatred was swallowed in love.
- Death was swallowed in victory.
- The cosmos was reclaimed for God.

The defining point of faith that makes us Christian (and more than conquerors) is that we believe the absurd message of the Cross. We believe the gospel of a crucified Messiah. To the unbelieving mind, such a claim is either a shameful scandal or utter nonsense. But, in fact, it is the power of God hidden in absurdity and disguised as foolishness. As we connect our faith with the Cross and its saving message, there flows from the Cross the reality of God's victory over sin, Satan, oppression, hatred, and death. The apostle Paul describes the great mystery of the Cross by saying that the wisest scholars or philosophers on earth do not know how to tell others how to know God. The wisdom of man is just plain foolishness to God. But God, in His great wisdom, has chosen to offer salvation to man through a message that appears to be foolishness—the message of the Cross. Paul says, "the foolishness of God is wiser than men, and the weakness of God is stronger than men."[17]

Paul told the Corinthians that he didn't come to them with just an excellent speech filled with persuasive words of human wisdom. He "determined not to know anything among you except Jesus Christ and Him crucified." He said he stood before them weak, fearful, and trembling, but "in demonstration of the Spirit and of power, that your faith should not be in the wisdom of men but in the power of God." He called the wisdom from God "a mystery, the hidden wisdom which God ordained before the ages for our glory, which none of the rulers of this age knew." If they had understood the mystery of God, "they would not have crucified the Lord of glory."[18]

In the event of the Cross, God turned conventional wisdom on its head. Everyone assumed that for Jesus to be the Messiah, He would have to do what the previous would-be messiahs had attempted to do: lead an armed revolution and kill the Romans and Herod. Instead, Jesus was put to a shameful death on a tree—and became King of the world! Yes, this is the true paradox of the Cross. Jesus is the true King of the Jews, whose crown was made of thorns, whose scepter was a reed, and whose coronation came through crucifixion. In due time, the Christian gospel of the Cross would conquer even the Roman Empire. This is the wisdom and power of God in a holy mystery.

The Position of Victory

Just because there is a moment in your life when it looks like the victory is lost and all hope is gone, remember the strange and absurd ways of God, and remember the death, burial, and resurrection of Jesus Christ. The three-act drama of death, burial, and resurrection is the central theme of the gospel story.

God intends to weave the same theme into your own story. So, on the worst day of your life, you may see nothing but death and burial, but don't forget act three. You are connected with Christ, and the dramatic conclusion of your story will be resurrection!

In reading Paul's epistles, it is abundantly clear that the apostle to the Gentiles was fascinated with God's victory over the powers of darkness through the enigma of the Cross. He likens the victory of the Cross to the victory parade of the Roman triumph, saying that God "always leads us in triumph in Christ, and through us diffuses the fragrance of His knowledge in every place."[19] Our triumphant God disarms "principalities and powers" and makes "a public spectacle of them, triumphing over them in it."[20]

Paul is comparing the victory of the Cross to a specific imperial practice that was well known at the time—the Roman triumph or victory parade. When a conquering Roman general returned to the capital city of Rome after a long and victorious campaign, he was given a great state-sponsored parade. The general would enter the city along the *Via Triumphalis*, and the whole city would turn out to witness the spectacle. Flower petals and incense were used in profusion to fill the air with the sweet smell of success. Musicians marched in the parade to sing the praises of the Roman gods and generals. The great general and his captains rode in royal chariots pulled by white horses, and the vanquished foes were led in chains through the streets of the city so everyone could clearly see they had been defeated.

This is exactly what Paul says has happened through the Cross! Jesus has triumphed over the enemies of God through His death, burial, and resurrection. Now He is entering His kingdom in a great victory parade. This is the kingdom of God. Jesus is crowned with many crowns, Satan and his demons are disarmed and publicly displayed as vanquished, and you and I are invited by the King Himself to march as more than conquerors in His own victory parade! This is the foundation for your own victory on the worst day of your life. No matter how bad things may seem, you are being led in triumph; you are in the victory parade of Christ Jesus.

So, it is from this position of victory in Christ that you launch your attack upon the powers of darkness that have seemingly robbed you. The truth is, Jesus is Lord, and the devil is defeated. The truth is, Christ is victorious, and Satan is vanquished. The truth is, Satan is disarmed, and you have the powerful weapons of the Word of God, the name of Jesus, the blood of Jesus, prayer and praise—all stemming from God's victory through the Cross of Christ. With this as your foundation, you can launch your attack on the powers of darkness.

Recover All

8

WHEN THE BATTLE was over and the victory secured, David and his men could finally relax. As they looked around the battleground, they saw the spoil the Amalekites had carried away from Ziklag. Their herds and flocks, their silver and gold—all of their possessions were there. Then from their hiding places, the women and children came running. As men sheathed their swords, little boys and girls jumped into their arms shouting, "Daddy!" Husbands and wives clung together in a joy-filled, tearful embrace. It must have been an incredible moment of unspeakable joy! It was a prophetic fulfillment. Thirty-six hours earlier, David had dared to utter these seemingly impossible words: "Recover all." Now the bold prophecy had been fulfilled.[1] They had recovered all.

The effect of the Fall, the reality of sin, the schemes of Satan, and the unexpected events of time and chance can seemingly rob life of meaning and joy, but there is a way in Christ to recover all. Life can deliver some very cruel blows. I've stood in hospital rooms and at gravesides with those who have seemingly lost all meaning for existence. I have prayed with those who have lost homes and businesses. I have felt the anguish in men who have lost their jobs and feel they have also lost their dignity. I have witnessed the pain of loss in parents who have seen their children abandon the faith. I have felt the pain of loss that comes from betrayal and deep disappointment in my own life. But I have also come to believe that there is a way—incredible as it may seem—to recover from the loss and pain you have suffered. You can recover from that devastating experience. You can recover your joy. You can recover from a financial failure. You can recover your dignity. You can recover your destiny. You can recover to the point where you once again enjoy a meaningful and fulfilling life. Yes, you may have suffered a tremendous loss, but in God there is recovery.

Don't let your personal tragedy or failure define your identity. Failure and loss are events, but they don't have to become an identity. Failure and loss are things that happen to you, but failure and loss are not who you are. Your identity is defined in Christ. In your mystical union with Christ you share in His death, burial, and resurrection. By faith you are united with the triumph of Christ—His triumph over sin, Satan, death, hell, and the grave. You may have been hurt, but you are not irrevocably broken. You may have been victimized, but you are not a perpetual victim. You may have suffered, but you are not a loser. You may have failed, but you are not a failure. Who are you? You are an overcomer in Christ. Overcomers recover. They may get knocked down, but they get back up. They may lose a battle, but they will win the war. They may suffer loss, but they will recover.

At its heart the story of David at Ziklag is a story of restoration, and at its heart, the story of the gospel is a story of restoration. Have you ever asked yourself, "What is salvation for?" Not what *is* salvation, but what is salvation *for*? Salvation is for the restoration of all things to God's original goodness. Salvation is the story of how God recovers from His loss.

God created a good world, but this good world was lost to sin, Satan, corruption, and death. The story the Bible tells is how God is in the process of recovering all that has been lost in the catastrophe of sin. This is the big picture of the Bible's story. God Himself knows what it is to suffer loss, and God also knows how to recover all.

Recovering All Is God's Plan

The Bible should read as a story, not primarily as a manual or a catalog. The Bible has a central storyline and is composed mostly of stories and subplots that move the grand narrative of Scripture forward (with a genealogy or a census thrown in here and there). The storyline of Scripture is told in the stories of Adam and Eve, Noah, Abraham, the patriarchs, Moses, David, Elijah, Jonah, the prophets and kings, the apostles and saints, and most of all, in the Gospel stories of Jesus. All of these stories are connected to one another in such a way as to tell the big-picture story of the Bible—the story of God's intention to recover all.

The story the Bible tells doesn't begin, "Once upon a time," because the story of the Bible begins before time. Instead, we read, "In the beginning God created the heavens and the earth."[2] As the Creation story progresses, we are told repeatedly that what God created, He called good. Upon completion of Creation, we are told that God declared it was all *very good*. In the creation of the physical universe and human society, God intended that creation might experience the goodness of God, but the story was to take a tragic turn.

I find it interesting that in the first two chapters of Genesis, the only punctuation needed are periods, commas, and some explanation points (*very good!*). But in chapter 3 of Genesis, a snake crawls into the garden, hissing his questions, and the twisted question mark makes its first appearance. Have you ever noticed that a question mark sort of resembles a snake? The twisted snake began to ask his twisted questions with the insidious intention of insinuating that God is perhaps not as good as He let on. You know how the story goes. What happened next we commonly call *the Fall*, and what a precipitous fall it was—a fall that would give the human race its legacy of sin, sorrow, war, injustice, pain, oppression, and seemingly endless loss. The end of this story would be sadder than any Greek tragedy.

But it's not the end of the story. Even before we leave the third chapter of Genesis, God speaks an encrypted prophecy about recovering all: "And I will put enmity between you and the woman, and between your seed and her Seed; He shall bruise your head, and you shall bruise His heel."[3]

God is no stranger to the horror and sorrow that David came upon when he returned to a ruined Ziklag. God is no stranger to the sorrow you have faced in your own devastating moments of loss. God is no stranger to loss. Think about it. God came into the Garden of Eden looking for fellowship with His image-bearing creatures and found His creation on fire, His world stolen, and His sons and daughters carried away captive. Did God weep? Perhaps. But what God certainly did was set in motion all that was necessary to eventually recover all.

Underlying all the familiar stories of the Bible—Noah's ark, Abraham's journey, Moses's exodus, David's kingdom, Elijah's miracles, Daniel's dreams—is the story of God's determination to recover all. The story of God's mission to restore all things to their original goodness reaches its climax in the coming of Messiah—the Seed of the woman who would bruise the serpent's head and recover all.

By the time Jesus was born in Bethlehem, the prophecies concerning Messiah had all been penned by the prophets and were well established in the consciousness and culture of the Jewish people. The nation of Israel languished under a succession of foreign oppressors: Babylonians, Persians, Greeks, and Romans. All of these regimes, like the Amalekites of David's day, had in their own way looted and plundered the Jewish nation. The national hopes were pinned on the coming of a prophesied Messiah, and by the time Augustus ruled Rome and Herod ruled Judea, the Jewish world was full of messianic expectations (not to mention the occasional messianic pretender, or false messiah).

In the first century A.D., Pharisees, Sadducees, Zealots, and Essenes were all expecting a messiah who would restore the fortunes of Israel and deliver them from the humiliating losses they had suffered under the domination of their various Gentile oppressors. The one thing all believing Jews had in common was the expectation of a Messiah who would be the King of the Jews and restore the lost glory of Israel. Their expectation was correct. What was incorrect was their assumption of how God would accomplish this.

Something I have learned over the years is that prophecy is not for prediction but for hope and glory. As the famous physicist Niels Bohr once humorously observed, "Prediction is very difficult, especially about the future."* The messianic oracles of the Hebrew prophets did not really enable the Jewish people to predict the details of their deliverer's, the Messiah's, coming. What these prophecies did was fill them with hope

---

* The Quotations Page, "Niels Bohr Quotes," http://www.quotationspage.com/quote/26159.html (accessed January 13, 2009).

and then, when the prophecies came to pass, enabled them to recognize what God had done and give Him glory.

When Jesus came riding into Jerusalem on the back of a donkey, the people remembered the prophecies of a Messiah that said, "Behold, your King is coming, sitting on a donkey's colt." They gathered branches of palm trees and went out to meet Him, crying out, "Hosanna! 'Blessed is He who comes in the name of the LORD!' The King of Israel!"[4] His disciples did not understand these things at first, but when Jesus was glorified, then they remembered that these things were written about Him and that they had done these things to Him.

What no one predicted—even though it was clearly prophesied—was that Messiah would deliver Israel and recover all—not by killing the Romans but by being crucified upon a Roman cross. Part of the glory of God is to fulfill all of His promises in a way that no one could have predicted. For example, the Old Testament law clearly stated that anyone who was hung upon a tree was cursed of God.[5]

Crucifixion was the standard Roman method for dealing with revolutionary messiahs (would-be kings who challenged the rule of Rome). Since the Torah stated that a crucified man was cursed of God, a crucified messiah was a failed messiah. But what if God raised a crucified messiah from the dead? This was the astounding claim that the first Jews who believed God had raised Jesus from the dead dared to make. They turned convention on its head by saying that, yes, Jesus had been hung upon a tree, but it was all part of God's plan to "recover all." They claimed that God had vindicated Jesus as the true Messiah by raising Him from the dead. After the Resurrection, the apostle Paul gave a new and deeper meaning to the Old Testament prophecy about a Messiah who would be hung from a tree and buried. He acknowledged the Jewish law that said anyone hanged from a tree was cursed but then revealed that by dying, Christ became "a curse for us," and by doing so, He opened the way of salvation to all people who would "receive the promise of the Spirit through faith."[6]

You Are God's Restoration Project

Through the Cross, God recovered all—for Himself, for humanity, for creation. God will restore all things through the death, burial, and resurrection of Jesus Christ. This is the great mystery of the Cross. What appears to be a curse becomes a blessing; what appears to be death becomes eternal life; what appears to be shame becomes glory; what appears to be defeat becomes victory; what appears to be loss becomes the restoration of all things.

The apostle Paul looked upon the Cross in the light of the Resurrection and saw what no one could have predicted: through the death, burial, and resurrection of His Son, Jesus, God our Father was able to "reconcile all things to Himself"—including things on earth and things in heaven.[7]

Throughout Jesus's three-year ministry, Peter seemed to excel in misunderstanding how Jesus would accomplish His mission. He regularly seemed to think that Jesus would restore

Israel's glory though conventional means, and he famously attempted to rebuke Jesus for talking about being crucified. After the resurrection and ascension of Jesus and the outpouring of the Holy Spirit, Peter finally came to understand that through Christ, God was restoring all of creation, not just the nation of Israel! He came to the realization that God had done so through the most improbable of means: the death of Messiah upon a cross.

A few weeks after the Resurrection, Peter and John healed a crippled beggar at the temple entrance by the authority of Jesus's name. Then Peter addressed a crowd in Solomon's porch, explaining to them how God is restoring all things through a crucified Messiah. He reminded them of the hopeful prophecies of a coming Messiah and boldly announced that "those things which God foretold by the mouth of all His prophets, that the Christ would suffer, He has thus fulfilled."[8] He called on all who were listening to "repent therefore and be converted, that your sins may be blotted out, so that times of refreshing may come from the presence of the Lord, and that He may send Jesus Christ, who was preached to you before, whom heaven must receive until the times of restoration of all things, which God has spoken by the mouth of all His holy prophets since the world began."[9]

Adam and Eve made a disastrous choice in the garden. They listened to the voice of the deceiver, the serpent, and decided they could define good and evil for themselves apart from God. That choice brought about universal catastrophe—the introduction of sin and death into God's good creation. But

God was not going to give up on His good creation; He was determined to recover all. Through the mysterious victory of the Cross, God is accomplishing what the apostle Peter calls the restoration of all things. The recovery of all things! What is salvation for? Salvation is for the restoration of all things to God's original goodness.

By your faith in Christ Jesus you are united with God's great restoration project. By your faith in the Cross of Christ the restorative power of redemption flows into your life. By your faith in the death, burial, and resurrection of the Son of God, you are connected through God's grace to recover all. In a world of loss and disappointment, it is faith that believes a crucified carpenter from Nazareth is the risen Son of God that will enable you to overcome the world of loss and disappointment and bring you to a place where you can truly say you have recovered all.

"Whatever is born of God overcomes the world." It is our faith in Jesus Christ and His work at Calvary that makes us overcomers. If we believe that Jesus Christ is the Son of God, we can overcome the world. [10]

You may have been hit by what feels like the worst day of your life. A twenty-first-century version of raiding Amalekites may have brought ruin to your hopes and dreams. It might be a lost job, a failed business, a foreclosure, a bankruptcy, a betrayal, a divorce, a wayward child, or even the death of a child. These are the kinds of losses that can seem impossible to recover from, but there is recovery. There is a grace that flows from the Cross to bring recovery into your life. Will you dare to speak outlandish words of faith? In the face of bitter loss can you say, "I will recover"? Will you dare to say, "I will recover all"?

You don't have to know how it will happen. You don't have to know when it will happen. You don't have to feel like it's true. It doesn't have to make sense to you. It is the absurd nature of faith to believe what appears to be impossible. I like what the early church father Tertullian said: "I believe because it is absurd."* You don't have to justify your faith to reason. Faith needs no other justification than the resurrection of Jesus. The resurrection of the Son of God is the cornerstone for every hope of recovery. It is a tried stone, a precious cornerstone, a sure foundation.[11]

You have every right to say, "I believe I will recover all because God raised His Son to life again." How will you recover from the loss of a job, a home, a friendship, a marriage, a child? I don't know. But I do know that God's grace is able to do far above all that we can ask or think according to the power of His grace at work in our lives.

So, this is my prophecy to you in the day of your loss: Maintain your faith in Jesus Christ, and you will recover all. I can't predict how or when, but I can tell you that faith will find a way, and you will recover. Your path to recovering all will probably come in a surprising way. God is full of such surprises. God maintains His faithfulness in fulfilling

---

* Tertullian, *Flesh*, 5 Ante-Nicene Fathers, Vol. 3, 525. Available online at http://phoenicia.org/tertullian2.html#n23 (accessed January 13, 2009).

His promises, but He maintains His sovereignty in surprise. So, even though it is incongruous, I will say, expect to be surprised! In the meantime, let the prophetic promise of recovery flood your soul with hope. When God brings to pass your surprising recovery, give Him glory. He is "able to do exceedingly abundantly above all that we ask or think, according to the power that works in us."[12] He deserves our glory—"forever and ever."

Celebrate Recovery

D AVID HAD RECOVERED all. He had recovered his flocks and herds, he had recovered his silver and gold, and he had recovered his family. What a joyful reunion it must have been. What a happy day it surely was. David had been to the brink of disaster. He had stared into the awful abyss, but through faith in Jehovah, David had, against all odds, recovered everything. If this were the end of the story, it would be a happy ending indeed, but this is not the end of the story.

As David looked around the camp of the Amalekites, he realized there was an abundance of spoil that had not come from Ziklag. The Amalekites had their own flocks and herds; they had their own silver and gold, but though the Amalekites were gone, their stuff was still there. David looked at the vast amount of Amalekite wealth and made this declaration: "This is David's spoil!"[1]

In an amazing twist of fate, David actually came out of the Ziklag catastrophe enriched. He had more than he had before. Such are the ways of God when satanic calamity encounters divine grace. The worst day of your life can become the catalyst for a better tomorrow. That which was designed to destroy you can actually bless you. You can do more than just survive the satanic assault; you can be catapulted into a new dimension of grace. The hideous ordeal you are going through now can become the stepping-stones to greater blessing in your life. No one can predict how such things can happen; it's just something a good and omniscient God can do. The Amalekites never imagined that their attack on David would enrich him, just as the principalities and powers could never have imagined that the crucifixion of Jesus would lead to His glory and the liberation of the world. God has a wonderful sense of irony in turning the tables on demonic intentions. Such unexpected reversals of fortune bring great glory to the mystery of God's wisdom. What a glorious mystery it is! "Eye has not seen, nor ear heard, nor have entered into the heart of man the things which God has prepared for those who love Him."[2]

The ways of God are such that when grace has accomplished its full work, we don't just recover, but we also celebrate recovery. Celebrate Recovery is a program that was begun in Rick Warren's Saddleback Church to help people who are struggling with, as they like to say, "hurts, habits, and hang-ups." We have a Celebrate Recovery ministry in our church. I love this ministry. I love the name: Celebrate Recovery! I've seen people who have suffered tremendous loss through substance abuse recover all and come to a place in life that is better than what they knew before their life was so devastated by addiction. There are many people for whom the struggle to overcome the demons of addictions became a catalyst for full liberation in Christ. These people didn't just recover sobriety, but they also discovered a life better than they had ever known before. They don't just recover; they celebrate recovery.

I see this in the spoils of David following the Ziklag disaster. I find near the conclusion of David's Ziklag story not just recovery but also a celebration of recovery. David was attacked, suffered loss, and then recovered all. But this is not the end. In the end, David was enriched with the spoils of his astounding comeback victory. David ended up with more than he had before.

Don't Underestimate God's Grace

You should never underestimate God's grace. Grace is God's chief means of delightful surprise, healing hurts, restoring the dance, and recovering beauty. Grace is the primary means by which God displays His glory in a fallen world. You should never underestimate the ability of God's grace to turn mourning into dancing or ashes into beauty. The psalmist cried out to God in pure joy by saying, "You have turned for

me my mourning into dancing; You have put off my sack-
cloth and clothed me with gladness, to the end that my glory
may sing praise to You and not be silent. O LORD my God, I
will give thanks to You forever."[3] Through the glorious grace
of God, we can "proclaim the acceptable year of the LORD,
and the day of vengeance of our God; to comfort all who
mourn."[4]

Mourning turned to dancing. Ashes turned to beauty.
These are astounding expressions of the greatness of God's
grace. Your worst days are prime candidates to become
the source of lavish grace and transcendent mercy. In the
moment, the worst day of your life is all about mourning
and anguish, ashes and ugliness. But because we are people
of faith, because we dare to believe in God when all seems
lost, the present devastation is not permitted to write the final
epitaph of your life. When human faith connects with divine
grace, there will ultimately be a celebration of recovery. A
celebration of recovery is what happens when mourning gives
way to dancing, and from the ashes of loss arises the beautiful
phoenix of God's grace.

When David first encountered his worst day, it seemed
that tears and ashes would be his final legacy, that his life
would be defined by tragedy. The ashes were undeniable,
and the tears were uncontrollable, but they were not David's
legacy; they were not what would ultimately define David.
The tears and the ashes are part of the story but not the whole
story. By the time the story was done, mourning had become

dancing (I'm sure David danced!), and from the ashes something beautiful arose.

The true spoil of David's recovery is not that he had a few more sheep or a little more silver. The true spoil of David's recovery is that three thousand years later we are still telling his story. In David's story we see the beauty of God's grace and find hope for our own troubled situations. From the ashes of Ziklag comes an inspiring story of recovery that is still being told three millennia later. This is beautiful.

Beauty is the final objective of God's gracious work, and ashes seem to be His favorite medium. God is the creator of beauty and a connoisseur of all that is truly beautiful. God is an artist, His canvas is creation, and in our lives tears and ashes are often His oil and clay as He works relentlessly to make something beautiful.

The whole story of Creation—the Fall and redemption—can be told in terms of beauty. We have an aesthetic gospel. God created man to be beautiful—to be a work of art. Man's sole purpose in Eden was to enjoy fellowship with God and cultivate beauty. The Fall was not only a breach of fellowship with our Creator, but it was also a descent into ugliness. So much of the human story is told with ugly words like *envy*, *hate*, *murder*, *war*, and *greed*. Man has lost much of his original beauty but not his love of art and his longing for beauty. That longing for beauty is a hidden longing for redemption, a cry to be saved from the ugliness of sin that has marred every human and left a deep scar upon creation. It's a cry for a Savior. We all have the desire to be beautiful again. This is not necessarily a vain, narcissistic desire, but in a much deeper way, it's the desire to recover our original state as beings who are intended to bear the image of God.

If God is an artist, then Satan is a vandal—a vandal intent upon defacing the image of God that humanity was created to bear.

In 1499, Michelangelo completed his masterpiece sculpture of the *Pietà*, a marble sculpture in Saint Peter's Basilica in Rome. The sculpture depicts the body of Jesus in the lap of His mother following His death upon the cross. The *Pietà* is a masterpiece that the art scholars tell us perfectly captures the Renaissance ideals of classical beauty balanced with naturalism. In 1972, a deranged vandal attacked the *Pietà* with a sledgehammer, raining fifteen blows upon it while shouting, "I am Jesus Christ!" Before the man could be restrained, he was able to inflict substantial damage upon the *Pietà*.*

The world was shocked, and for a time, it was feared that an irreplaceable masterpiece had been lost to a senseless act of vandalism. But the restoration artists were convinced that the *Pietà* could be saved, and within twelve months, it had been restored to its original beauty. A few years ago my wife and I saw this great work of art, and I can bear witness that it's not only a testimony to the genius of Michelangelo, but it is also a testimony to the skills of the restoration artists who

---

* St. Peter's Basilica, "Chapel of the Pietà," http://www.saintpetersbasilica.org/Altars/Pieta/Pieta.htm (accessed January 13, 2009).

were able to fully recover its lost beauty. The *Pietà* is not just a celebration of beauty; it is now a celebration of recovery.

Celebrate Recovery

Jesus is a restoration artist. He came to restore to beauty a humanity vandalized by a deranged fallen angel who attacked our race. With a sledgehammer of deceit, Satan wielded vicious blows upon God's masterpiece, and the human race appeared to be marred beyond recovery. Our gospel proclaims that on the cross Jesus absorbed the ugliness of human sin and the violence of satanic assault into His own body and turned sin and violence into the beauty of salvation.

This miracle is testified to by the very image of the cross itself. Originally the cross was a hideous spectacle that caused people to turn away in revulsion and horror. But now the cross has become an image of beauty depicted as a work of art in countless ways. Jesus transformed the cross from ugliness to beauty. This is precisely what Jesus wants to do with humanity—turn ugliness into beauty. We have an aesthetic gospel.

The storyline of something ugly being turned into something beautiful, which is so common in literature (such as *Cinderella* and *The Ugly Duckling*), is a familiar genre in Scripture. We see it in the life of David, in the stories of the patriarchs, and perhaps most clearly of all in the life of Joseph. Joseph was the dreamer, the eleventh of Jacob's twelve sons. He dreamed of greatness, was favored by his father, and was the wearer of the beautiful coat of many colors. But the ugliness of jealousy, rivalry, and envy led to many ugly events and ugly years in Joseph's life. Betrayed by his brothers, thrown into a pit, sold into slavery, and purported to be dead, Joseph found himself living an ugly life. There were times when he would seem to be rising above the ugliness of betrayal and slavery, only to be lied about once more and thrown into prison so that the ugly cycle would begin again. But Joseph held fast to his hopes and dreams, and he held fast to his faith and integrity. After thirteen long years, Joseph suddenly rose above the ugliness of injustice to become the prime minister of Egypt. Who could have predicted that?

If the story ended here it would be a morality tale of a good man preserving and overcoming against all odds. But, of course, the story does not end with Joseph's promotion. Nine years after Joseph had become second only to Pharaoh, his brothers came to Egypt in search of grain during a devastating famine. When Joseph finally revealed himself to his astonished and terrified brothers, he forgave them and reassured them with these amazing words: "Do not be afraid, for am I in the place of God? But as for you, you meant evil against me; but God meant it for good, in order to bring it about as it is this day, to save many people alive. Now therefore, do not be afraid; I will provide for you and your little ones."[5] And he comforted them and spoke kindly to them.

Joseph acknowledges that his brothers' intent was evil, but he also acknowledges that God was able to use what was intended for evil to bring about good. Thus, the beauty of reconciliation was born out of the ugliness of betrayal.

Furthermore, and more importantly, Joseph's sojourn in slavery resulted in the salvation of the entire household of Israel, who otherwise may have perished in the great famine. It is in stories like these that we understand how the sovereign grace of God can work with the most horrible events to bring about something good. All of these stories are but echoes of what God accomplished at Calvary and the garden tomb when He turned the mourning of Good Friday into the dancing of Easter Sunday.

On the worst day of your life you can never predict how God will bring about recovery, much less how God will make something worth celebrating out of the ugly ashes that have come to dominate your present. But He will. Believe this. Put your trust in the God who specializes in turning mourning into dancing and ashes into beauty. Your beautiful days of dancing are yet to come. You cannot predict how or when, but you can believe it. Faith never underestimates the potential of grace. Joseph could never have predicted how something beautiful would come out of betrayal and slavery, but he found a way to hold on to his dreams and dared to believe that God had not forgotten or forsaken him.

In my own life, I have found that the times that were most painful and undesirable, the times when I was tempted to quit or run away, have eventually become the matrix for a whole new realm of blessing and breakthrough. The pain of betrayal and disappointment proved to be the hammer and chisel of God's grace as He sculpted something out of my life far more beautiful than I could have imagined. The hammer and chisel may have indeed been painful events, even events intended by the evil one for work of destruction, but in the hands of God they became tools of beauty, amazing grace, and holy mystery!

"If it seems too good to be true, it probably is." This is sage advice that is nearly always true, except when we are speaking of the grace of God. God's chief means of filling the earth with His glory in a world gone wrong is to bring about unfathomable goodness from unbearable tragedy. Only God can do this. Thus, it serves the glory of God. It is an astounding discovery to find that the devil at his worst ultimately only serves to further the glory of God. This is true on a global scale, and it is true on the personal level—if you can by faith attach yourself to the grace of God.

The apostle Paul observed that "where sin abounded, grace abounded much more, so that as sin reigned in death, even so grace might reign through righteousness to eternal life through Jesus Christ our Lord."[6]

Faith is the audacity to believe such outrageous claims— that unfathomable goodness can come from unbearable tragedy. Faith is the audacity to believe that when you have lost it all, you will not only recover all, but you will also live to celebrate recovery. Faith is the audacity to believe that in the midst of the ashes of ruin you will again dance for joy.

Tell yourself this. Dare to believe it. Take the leap of faith. Let faith fly in the face of reason, and courageously proclaim that you will dance again, that you will celebrate recovery, that beauty will come forth from the ashes of loss, and that in the end you will be better off than before! I know this isn't easy. This is not common faith; this is audacious faith, exceptional faith. It is the heroic faith of Hebrews chapter 11. But I also know you are capable of it. You are capable of it because the Word of God can produce it, and the Holy Spirit will help you. Audacious faith lies within the capacity of the exceptional choice. You are capable of making the exceptional choice of audacious faith to believe that you will not only recover, but that you will also celebrate recovery.

Give to Others

D AVID AND HIS men loaded up the spoil from their great victory over the Amalekites and returned with their families and possessions to Ziklag. The amount of wealth that had been taken from the Amalekites was staggering, far more wealth than David had ever possessed. What David did with that wealth reveals why he was such a great man and why God called him, "a man after My own heart."[1] David gave an offering from this spoil.[2]

David was not merely interested in getting rich and filling his own coffers, as were so many petty chieftains in the land of Canaan. David had more vision than that. David had a giving spirit, and he wanted to bless others. David made a list of his friends who were among the elders of Judah, at least thirteen of them. David prepared thirteen generous offerings of cattle, sheep, silver, and gold. Then he selected trusted men to take these offerings to the various elders in their various cities. David told his men to say, "Here is a present for you from the spoil of the enemies of the Lord." David also sent offerings to those who had befriended him during the time of his exile. David delighted in blessing his friends and giving to others, which is not always a common trait for those who come into great wealth.

When the men arrived in each one of the cities of Judah with the offerings of sheep, cattle, silver, and gold, they inquired for the elders of the city. Then they ceremoniously presented them with these gifts from David. Of course there was tremendous joy in the city. Since the days of Moses—for five hundred years—the Amalekites had harassed the Israelites. But now David had taken the wealth of the Amalekites and used it to bless and strengthen the people of God.

Three days after David sent these offerings, King Saul was killed in battle on Mount Gilboa. Shortly after that, David was installed as king of Judah. It should not be overlooked how quickly David's situation totally changed! The Bible uses the word *suddenly* again and again. Hard times can seem to go on endlessly, but when God turns things around, it can be overnight. Now things had really turned around for David. Fifteen years after Samuel had anointed David to be king, David at last came to the throne. But it happened just a few days after he had selflessly given.

Is there a connection? I suspect so. Saul had proven himself to be greedy and covetous, and God had regretted making him king. But David had proven he had a different spirit—David had a generous and giving spirit. David wanted to bless the people of Israel, not use and exploit them. David's final act before ascending to the throne was to give to others. So the story of Ziklag does not end with David getting back what had been stolen. The story does not end with David possessing the spoil of the Amalekites. The story ends with David giving to others and being promoted by God to his prophetic destiny.

When we encounter hard times, when we face the worst day of our life, it is very easy to become self-absorbed. Our crisis can very easily become our entire universe. When we are facing a soul-crushing tragedy, we can even be offended that the birds go on singing as if everything were normal. We want to shout at the birds, "Stop it! This is no time for singing!" When we are in the midst of a terrible personal crisis, we want the whole world to stop and take notice. Of course it does not. The world goes on.

On the other hand, when we come through hard times and are gloriously delivered from the worst day of our life and are now elated with happiness, we can make the mistake of thinking that the whole world should be rejoicing. We can think that every funeral should be canceled and every tear should be dried because something good has happened to us. But the funerals are not canceled, and the tears of those who are just now entering their worst day continue to be shed. Life goes on.

What we need to learn is that we are not the center of the universe. We are created by God, known by God, loved by God. God takes a personal interest in our lives; God Himself shares in our joys and sorrows, but God does not build the universe around us. If we try to make self the center of our own personal universe, disaster results.

Beware—Black Holes

Perhaps the most fearsome objects in the physical universe are black holes. A black hole is an immense star that no longer has the capacity to sustain itself. It collapses in upon itself, creating a gravitational pull from which not even light can escape. This is the problem of being the center of your own universe but not having enough energy or substance to sustain your function as a star—you collapse in upon yourself and become a black hole. Strangely enough, Jude seems to make a kind of reference to black holes when he talks about those who pretend to be a part of us but are in reality just serving themselves. He calls them "clouds without water, carried about by the winds; late autumn trees without fruit, twice dead, pulled up by the roots; raging waves of the sea, foaming up their own shame; wandering stars for whom is reserved the blackness of darkness forever."[3]

These wandering stars who serve only themselves and refuse to be a part of any other orbit become doomed to the blackness of darkness forever. Black holes are scary stuff! These spooky phenomena that exist in outer space may well be parallels for humans who refuse to allow God to have His way in their lives. The only way to prevent orbiting around yourself and ending up a doomed black hole is to have something other than self at the center of your personal universe and to learn to properly relate to other people.

Greed, avarice, and self-centeredness lead only to death by black hole—a lonely, dark existence where nothing exists but your own wretched self. Surely this has something to do with hell. The atheistic existentialist philosopher and playwright Jean-Paul Sartre famously quipped, "Hell is other people."* No, hell is not being able to *love* other people. If you don't learn to love other people, you will create hell before you go to hell.

Self cannot be at the center of our personal universe. This is the equation that in the end only adds up to hell. Only God has enough substance to be the object of endless orbit. We must build our lives around God and learn to properly relate to others. This is what worship and justice are all about. Worship is how we rightly relate to God; justice is how we rightly relate to other people. This is the divine purpose in the Ten Commandments. The intent of the Ten Commandments is to form the people of God into a worshiping and just society. The first four commandments order our worship: no other gods, no idols, don't be casual with God's name, and keep the sacred day sacred. The final six commandments order our interaction with other people: honor your parents, don't murder, don't commit adultery, don't steal, don't lie, and don't envy.

---

* Jean-Paul Sartre, *No Exit* (New York: Vintage Books, 1989), 45.

The two great sins that led to Israel's failure were idolatry and injustice, and they are inextricably related. Idolatry always leads to injustice; wrong worship always produces a wrong treatment of others. Likewise, it is impossible to worship acceptably if we don't treat our fellow human beings in a right manner. In the end, it all comes down to worship and justice.

I wonder about the lasting effect of Ziklag upon David. Did David emerge from the Ziklag disaster a more compassionate and giving person? Perhaps. I know in my own life that personal pain has served to make me more compassionate toward others. If we don't come through our struggles more committed to worship and justice, more grateful to God, and more compassionate toward others, what is the point? If I make the mistake of thinking that the point is just to get me out of my own personal Ziklag and nothing more, I am still on a trajectory that leads to a black hole. What a shame if our pain is wasted and we emerge from Ziklag fully restored but totally unchanged. This must not be. We must allow the experiences of Ziklag to transform us into greater givers.

Pay It Forward

The only thing greater than recovering all by the grace of God is to be an agent of God's grace in the lives of others, helping them to recover all. To do this we must be givers. We must be willing to give generously, even sacrificially. We must move beyond obsession with our own joy or sorrow and acknowledge the significance of others. We must truly "love our neighbor as ourselves," which is the second commandment and is inexorably linked to the first commandment, to love the Lord our God will all our heart, soul, mind, and strength. We do this by doing our best to insure that others have what they need:

- Money
- Food
- Shelter
- Compassion
- Respect
- Dignity
- Time
- Assistance
- Employment
- Counsel
- Friendship
- Love

We give from the spoils of our own personal experiences with the grace of God. If we fail to do this, we have squandered the grace of God and are moving in the direction of a black hole.

Sometimes I suspect that God allows painful experiences into our lives so that we can understand and help alleviate the pain of others. Somehow our suffering becomes a form of redemptive suffering so that, like Jesus, we can be men and women of sorrows and acquainted with grief, not merely as an exercise in empathy but so that we might have a genuine capacity to give restorative grace to others. Do you know from personal experience the pain of poverty, the agony of addiction, the devastation of divorce, the knife wound of betrayal, the embarrassment of bankruptcy, the despair of failure, the soul-crushing ache of real loss? Has God by His grace brought you beyond that painful past? Be sure of this, He did not do it for your sake alone but that you might be an agent of redeeming grace in the lives of others.

Among the remarkable escapades of the Old Testament judge and deliverer Samson was the extraordinary experience of being attacked by a lion. I imagine that could be an unpleasant experience, but we are told the Spirit of the Lord came upon Samson, and he tore the lion to pieces, though he had nothing in his hands. Needless to say, that is the grace of God. A few days later, Samson returned to the place where the lion had attacked him and found that a swarm of bees had formed a hive in the carcass of the lion. From the lion, Samson filled his hands with honey and went and gave some to his parents. I like that. When the lion attacked, Samson was empty-handed, but now he has hands full of honey. What a sweet testimony. Notice that Samson didn't keep the honey all for himself; he gave it to others. Samson even formed a riddle from this episode. "Out of the eater came something to eat, and out of the strong came something sweet."[4]

It is a riddle because it is a paradox the powers of evil just can't quite comprehend. How is it that their attack makes us stronger? How is it that their attempt to bring bitterness results in sweetness? How is it that pulling us down brings us up higher? The grace of God often appears in a paradoxical way. No doubt the intent of the lion was to devour Samson, but in the end, Samson got something to eat. By all rights, when the lion attacked, Samson's life should have come to a swift and bitter end, but it turned out to bring sweetness into Samson's life—a sweetness that he was quick to share with others.

It is the value of giving to others that is the final lesson to learn from what David did on the worst day of his life. David didn't just recover and celebrate; David thought about others, considered others, and gave to others. The grace of God that enables you to recover all is not to end in your life alone, so that you become a kind of Dead Sea of unrequited blessing. Instead, the grace to recover all is to flow through your life, bringing help, hope, and healing to other people. Remember, Ziklag is not Bethlehem, the place of beginnings, and neither is it Jerusalem, the place of completion. It is somewhere in between. It is the place that appears ordinary one day, horrific the next, and can somehow then become the place of a tremendous testimony of recovery. Even when recovery and celebration become realities, Ziklag is still not the final destination. Recovery and celebration are not ends in themselves. You are called to be and do things that no one else can be or do. The sooner you can learn to look beyond your own sorrows and joys and find ways to connect with others by giving to them from what you have, the sooner you will begin to fulfill the purposes appointed by God for your life.

A Tapestry of Grace

D AVID WAS A remarkable man, an Old Testament Renaissance man, a shepherd and a psalmist, a poet and a prophet, a warrior and a king, and most of all, a man of divine destiny. Here is a humble shepherd boy who was chosen by God to reign as a king and shepherd a nation—chosen because God liked what He saw when He looked into his heart. David was a remarkable man because he didn't give up and quit in a time of seeming disaster. Instead, he found a way in God to press on and overcome, even when it seemed to be the worst day of his life.

Because of his faith and perseverance, David fulfilled his destiny and reigned as Israel's greatest king for forty years, even becoming a prophecy of the greater messianic King who would also be born in Bethlehem and would also be crowned in Jerusalem, albeit with a crown of thorns. Yes, Bethlehem was the place of David's beginning, the place of prophecy, and Jerusalem was the place where David reigned, the place of destiny. But between the Bethlehem beginning and the Jerusalem destiny, David had to overcome the Ziklag trial.

In many respects, the life of David is given to us as an inspirational pattern, a kind of template by which we can interpret some of the events in our own lives. God's good intention is that we should reign in life, that we should learn how to worship God and serve others as a kingdom of priests. It is a long journey to reach the place in life where you are actually becoming the person you were meant to be—even as it was for David.

You have begun the journey. You may well have experienced your own Bethlehem beginning, where you first began to sense there really is a greater purpose, even a prophetic destiny for your life. Perhaps now you sense that you are somehow on your way to Jerusalem, the place of destiny, where the purposes of God are fulfilled in your life and you reign as a king in order to serve others. But between Bethlehem and Jerusalem there are always Ziklags. Ziklag is unavoidable, not only because there are powers of darkness bent on our destruction, but also because, in a much deeper and more mysterious way, Ziklag is an essential part of our own personal development. Between prophecy and destiny there is always testing and refinement. God's purpose for allowing you to encounter Ziklag is not to hurt you or ruin you but to develop in you a kingly and gratuitous spirit so that you will be fit to rule and serve when you reach Jerusalem.

Ziklag may seem like the worst day of your life when you first encounter it, but as you walk by faith through the trial on your way toward the testimony of recovering all, Ziklag becomes the crucible where the precious possession of a fire-refined faith is developed in you. That's when Paul's famous declaration, "We are more than conquerors through Him who loved us," is no longer an empty religious cliché but a real-life experience.

When you encounter a Ziklag disaster in the course of your faith journey, David's story helps you know how to respond. Weep for a while, but don't get bitter. Encourage yourself, get a word from God, and reorient your vision. Recover your passion, attack the enemy, and recover all! Then, celebrate your recovery, and begin to look for opportunities to give to others. That's when you will have not only come full circle, but you will also have moved beyond Ziklag toward the kingly destiny of reigning in life by helping others. Over time (and it may be a long time), you can even gain a whole new perspective on the pain you have suffered. This is the final and greatest work of grace, and I like to describe it as a tapestry of grace. Let me explain.

We may be able to gain a certain perspective on our own time by looking back seven hundred years. Europe in 1300 was experiencing a boom of technological advance and economic success. The general prosperity of the late thirteenth century had imbued Europe with an air of optimism. Then all hell broke loose. Europe was hit by a series of disasters that seemed to come right out of the Book of Revelation. Economic collapse, climate change (the Little Ice Age), the Hundred Years' War, the Peasants' Revolt, widespread famine, and worst of all, the "black death" of bubonic plague. Europe was also under constant threat of Islamic invasion. This series of disasters threatened the basic social order of Europe and reduced the population by as much as a third. Those who were living through the horrors of the fourteenth century began to seriously question if they were witnessing the extinction of the human race. The general mood of the time was one of turmoil, diminished expectations, loss of confidence in institutions, and feelings of helplessness at forces beyond human control.

During this tumultuous time, there lived in Norwich, England, a Christian mystic known to us as Julian of Norwich. At the age of thirty, Julian received a series of divine visions while she was severely ill and near death. Upon her recovery she wrote a book based on the visions she had seen. The book is titled *Revelations of Divine Love* and is believed to be the first book written by a woman in the English language. *Revelations of Divine Love* is full of hope and optimism and became a profound source of comfort for those living through that disastrous time. In chapter 27, Julian of Norwich famously writes, "Sin is cause of all this pain, but all shall be well, and all shall be well."*

---

* Julian of Norwich, *Revelations of Divine Love* (New York: Cosimo, 2007), 27.

Everything Is Going to Be All Right

All shall be well. Or to put it in more common vernacular, I would say it this way: everything will be all right. I believe that. I believe everything will be all right. I believe it because it is a great promise from God Himself: "And we know that all things work together for good to those who love God, to those who are the called according to His purpose."[1]

To those of us living through the global challenges of the early twenty-first century, and to those who on a personal level are facing what you might call the worst day of your life, I want to say something: everything is going to be all right. I don't say this glibly or cheaply, but I say this with deep conviction and full assurance of faith. Everything is going to be all right. This is true because making everything all right is the greatest and final work of grace. For those to whom salvation is conferred in Jesus Christ, in the final end, everything is going to be all right. Despite the sin, the failure, the loss, the pain, the sorrow, the heartbreak…despite it all, everything really is going to be all right. Not because I say so, but because God has promised to make your life a tapestry of grace.

Are you familiar with tapestries? Tapestries are woven hangings often adorned with complex pictures that tell a story. Perhaps the most famous tapestry is the Bayeux tapestry in France. Not long ago, Peri and I saw this 230-foot-long tapestry, which tells in intricate detail the story of William the Conqueror and the Norman victory over King Harold and the Saxons in the Battle of Hastings in 1066. Nearly a thousand years later, this tapestry is still telling its story. In medieval times, tapestries were often used to decorate the walls of a royal palace. Our King wants to decorate His kingdom with tapestries of grace telling the life stories of those whom He has redeemed.

God is an artist and weaver, a maker of tapestries. Your life is a story that is to be told in tapestry. It is very instructive to understand that the artist creating the tapestry upon the loom works from the *back* of the tapestry. To fully appreciate this analogy, you must understand that the back of the tapestry is your story *in the present moment*. The front of the tapestry is the finished story, while the back of the tapestry is the story as it is being created. There are two sides to a tapestry: the back, where it is being created, and the front, which tells the completed story.

Have you ever looked at the back of a tapestry? What do you find? It is a mess of loose ends, tangled knots, muted colors, and general confusion. The front or finished side of the tapestry tells a beautiful story that makes perfect sense, while the back of the tapestry is a confusing and tangled mess that doesn't make any sense at all. Both sides use the same threads, but they produce different pictures. Or, if I can just come out and say it, much of what happens in the immediate moment doesn't seem at all beautiful and doesn't make much sense. In a present moment of crisis, our life just seems like a mess of loose ends and tangled knots, but when God completes His work, you will see the finished picture. It will all be beautiful, and everything will make sense. This is what it means for your life to be a tapestry of grace.

Sometimes in the present moment, in the thick of the battle, in times of personal crisis, our lives can seem to be discordant, bewildering, broken beyond repair. But never forget that the One who sits at the loom works with a creative hand skilled in the art of grace. Jeremiah the prophet described this artist as a potter, and I am describing Him as a weaver, but the message is the same: when you have surrendered your life to God's grace, your times are in God's hand. David said it this way: "But as for me, I trust you, O LORD; I say, 'You are my God.' My times are in Your hand."[2]

Consider again Paul's promise in Romans: "All things work together for good." Quite a remarkable statement. Very similar to what Julian of Norwich meant in saying, "All shall be well." It's what I mean when I say everything is going to be all right. "All things work together for good." All "things" are all *threads*. The things that happen are the threads of your life. Not every thread that comes into your life comes from God. Some threads come from God,[3] but some threads come from Satan.[4] Many threads come from our own choices.[5] Other threads are simply the result of time and chance.[6] But for those who love God and are called according to His purpose, God makes this promise: He will weave every thread into the tapestry of your life in such a way that in the end it tells a good and beautiful story. Or to use Paul's language, God causes all the threads of our lives to be woven together for good.

The apostle Paul makes a truly remarkable statement when he says, "If anyone loves God, this one is known by Him."[7] What a provocative sentence. Those who love God are known

time to time we hear a story that reminds us how
rk all things together for good.

Work Together for Good

ew up in a Christian home in London, where
prominent Methodist minister. No doubt
hoped and prayed that their son would
eir Christian faith. The young man was
ellectually and, as a boy, attended a school
odist ministers, founded by John Wesley,
ism. While at that school, Kingswood
and, a young Antony Flew began to
s parents. He tells the story himself in
ne I reached my fifteenth birthday, I
universe was created by an all-good,
ny Flew had become an atheist.
luate at Oxford, Flew attended
S. Lewis's Socratic Club, often
oncerning the existence of God.
he world's leading intellectual
works on atheism and often
emost "evangelist." Flew also
istian apologists in debates
, the resurrection of Jesus,
imagine the pain this had
were giving their lives in

One, 2007), 15.

by God. Is it possible for someone to be unknown to God?
Apparently. Jesus declares that in the final judgment some
will be told, "I never knew you."[8]

Love is not only a benevolent inclination; love is also a
form of knowledge. To love something is a way of knowing
it. Love is the highest form of knowledge, and in the end,
love is the only form of knowledge that really matters.[9] Ultimately, God will know only that which loves Him and that
which He loves. Hell must somehow be the place for all
things forgotten by God. But everything God knows, everything that loves God, will be made beautiful. This really is
the meaning of God's promise to make everything beautiful,
to make everything all right.

That gives us a profoundly altered perspective on the
present. Paul said he considered "that the sufferings of this
present time are not worthy to be compared with the glory
which shall be revealed in us."[10]

Our lives are comprised of an endless series of events. Think
of each event as a thread in the tapestry that is the story of
your life. Those events that are unpleasant to us are the coarse
and dark threads. But God promises to weave them into our
story in such a way that in the end everything will be all right.
It doesn't mean that everything is all right in the immediate
moment, but in the end your story will be perfect.

When God has completed His work on the tapestry of your
life and shows it to you, you will say it's perfect. What about
those coarse and dark threads that were so painful in the
present moment? They have been woven into the whole of the

tapestry in such a way that you won't want to change a thing. God doesn't remove the painful events from our past; God doesn't erase our memory. That would be dishonest. What God does is work the painful events into the story of our lives in such a way that they work out for good. As incredible as it may seem, someday you will be able to say with total honesty and conviction, "Nothing bad has ever happened to me." I believe that with all my heart.

Of course you can't say that now, but when God has completed His awesome work of grace, you will find that all things have worked out for your good. To believe this is a profound source of hope and comfort. When grace comes into your life through faith in Jesus Christ, it moves in every direction, even reaching back into your past and redeeming that which seemed so painful and destructive at the time.

Everything is going to be all right. This is the overarching message of the gospel. God is going to set right a world gone wrong, and God is going to set right what's gone wrong in your life. God deals in both immensity and minutia. As the supreme intelligence behind the laws of physics, God is the engineer of the universe, and He is interested in both cosmology (the study of the very, very large) and quantum mechanics (the study of the very, very small).

God Has a Plan for You

God's interest in the whole range of astrophysics is nothing compared to God's interest in the whole range of human experience. God is concerned about His creation on a cosmic

scale and on the person of creation through the concerned about the even to the extent head.[12] God has plan to take ca

So we con God's Wor epistle to and all thing Go ir

good. From God can wo

All Thing

Antony Flew gr his father was Antony's parents follow them in t extremely gifted in for children of Meth the father of Metho School in Bath, Eng abandon the faith of h this manner: "By the ti rejected the thesis that th all-powerful God."* Anto Later as an undergra the weekly meetings of C engaging Lewis in debates Flew went on to become atheist, publishing some forty being described as atheism's fo regularly engaged leading Chr concerning the existence of Go and life after death. We can only to cause his Christian parents, wh

* Antony Flew, There Is a God (New York: Harp

Goα

Christian ministry. We can only imagine how they continued to pray for their son.

In 2007, I was returning from India and was changing planes in New York. During the brief layover I walked into an airport bookstore to find some reading material for the final flight home. While browsing in the philosophy section, a book caught my eye: *There Is a God: How the World's Most Notorious Atheist Changed His Mind* by (you guessed it!) Antony Flew. I was stunned! I bought the book and read the whole thing on my flight back to Kansas City. It's probably the best apologetic work I've ever read on defending the existence of God. But it's more than just an argument for the existence of God; it is a fascinating autobiographical story of Flew's long, slow journey from atheism to belief in God.

Antony Flew is now eighty-five years old, and his parents have long since died. But their prayers live on—prayers that have now been answered. The strange and wonderful thing is, Antony Flew will probably end up doing more to bring people to belief in God through his late-in-life conversion following a lifetime of atheism than if he had followed his father into Christian ministry. I'm not suggesting that God was responsible for Antony Flew's atheism—I don't believe that—but I am suggesting that this is a marvelous example of God working all things together for good. I suspect Antony Flew's Methodist parents would agree.

How bad a day was it for Reverend and Mrs. Flew when their son announced that he had become an atheist? Could it perhaps have been the worst day of their lives? But that wasn't the end of the story. Antony Flew's parents did not live to see the answer to their prayers, but their prayers have been answered nonetheless, and in some strange mystical way we really can't understand right now, I believe that this couple will one day indeed rejoice. They will laugh with joy, they will give praise to their God, and they will shake their heads as they wonder and marvel over the incredible power of God to turn their story around.

Could it be people like Reverend and Mrs. Flew whom the writer of Hebrews is referring to in Hebrews 11 when he writes, "These all died in faith, not having received the promises, but having seen them afar off were assured of them"?[14]

In this life we will have some bad days. Some may be so bad that recovery seems impossible, but all things are possible to him who believes. On the worst day of your life, perhaps the best thing you can do is remember this promise: "All things work together for good," and dare to believe that this too will work out for good and that somehow everything is going to be all right. Remember, your times are in God's hand. He is the artist who has promised to weave all things in such a way that in the end your story will truly be a story of beauty, a work of art, God's masterpiece that can never be marred or touched, His beautiful tapestry of grace.

by God. Is it possible for someone to be unknown to God? Apparently. Jesus declares that in the final judgment some will be told, "I never knew you."[8]

Love is not only a benevolent inclination; love is also a form of knowledge. To love something is a way of knowing it. Love is the highest form of knowledge, and in the end, love is the only form of knowledge that really matters.[9] Ultimately, God will know only that which loves Him and that which He loves. Hell must somehow be the place for all things forgotten by God. But everything God knows, everything that loves God, will be made beautiful. This really is the meaning of God's promise to make everything beautiful, to make everything all right.

That gives us a profoundly altered perspective on the present. Paul said he considered "that the sufferings of this present time are not worthy to be compared with the glory which shall be revealed in us."[10]

Our lives are comprised of an endless series of events. Think of each event as a thread in the tapestry that is the story of your life. Those events that are unpleasant to us are the coarse and dark threads. But God promises to weave them into our story in such a way that in the end everything will be all right. It doesn't mean that everything is all right in the immediate moment, but in the end your story will be perfect.

When God has completed His work on the tapestry of your life and shows it to you, you will say it's perfect. What about those coarse and dark threads that were so painful in the present moment? They have been woven into the whole of the tapestry in such a way that you won't want to change a thing. God doesn't remove the painful events from our past; God doesn't erase our memory. That would be dishonest. What God does is work the painful events into the story of our lives in such a way that they work out for good. As incredible as it may seem, someday you will be able to say with total honesty and conviction, "Nothing bad has ever happened to me." I believe that with all my heart.

Of course you can't say that now, but when God has completed His awesome work of grace, you will find that all things have worked out for your good. To believe this is a profound source of hope and comfort. When grace comes into your life through faith in Jesus Christ, it moves in every direction, even reaching back into your past and redeeming that which seemed so painful and destructive at the time.

Everything is going to be all right. This is the overarching message of the gospel. God is going to set right a world gone wrong, and God is going to set right what's gone wrong in your life. God deals in both immensity and minutia. As the supreme intelligence behind the laws of physics, God is the engineer of the universe, and He is interested in both cosmology (the study of the very, very large) and quantum mechanics (the study of the very, very small).

God Has a Plan for You

God's interest in the whole range of astrophysics is nothing compared to God's interest in the whole range of human experience. God is concerned about His creation on a cosmic scale and on the personal level. God intends to redeem all of creation through the work of the Cross,[11] and God is also concerned about the tiny episodes in your individual life, even to the extent that He bothers to count the hairs on your head.[12] God has a plan to redeem the cosmos, and God has a plan to take care of you. Everything is going to be all right.

So we continue to pray, to trust God, to build our faith on God's Word, to frame our worldview from Paul's masterpiece epistle to the Romans (especially chapter 8), and, despite any and all evidence to the contrary, we dare to believe that everything is going to be all right. We do this because we believe God is in charge and that He loves us and has promised to intervene in our lives with love and grace. Of this the apostle Paul was certain. He was firmly and absolutely "persuaded that neither death nor life, nor angels nor principalities nor powers, nor things present nor things to come, nor height nor depth, nor any other created thing, shall be able to separate us from the love of God which is in Christ Jesus our Lord."[13]

Of course we want everything to be all right *now*. This is our common human experience. But because everything is not all right in the present moment, we are prone to panic and forget the promise. So remember this: In this present moment, you are enveloped in the love of God in Christ Jesus. Right now there is nothing that can separate you from that love. Everything is going to be all right, but the work of making everything all right may take some time. So, having believed the promise of God, you simply wait in hope for God to keep His promise and work all things together for good. From time to time we hear a story that reminds us how God can work all things together for good.

All Things Work Together for Good

Antony Flew grew up in a Christian home in London, where his father was a prominent Methodist minister. No doubt Antony's parents hoped and prayed that their son would follow them in their Christian faith. The young man was extremely gifted intellectually and, as a boy, attended a school for children of Methodist ministers, founded by John Wesley, the father of Methodism. While at that school, Kingswood School in Bath, England, a young Antony Flew began to abandon the faith of his parents. He tells the story himself in this manner: "By the time I reached my fifteenth birthday, I rejected the thesis that the universe was created by an all-good, all-powerful God."* Antony Flew had become an atheist.

Later as an undergraduate at Oxford, Flew attended the weekly meetings of C. S. Lewis's Socratic Club, often engaging Lewis in debates concerning the existence of God. Flew went on to become the world's leading intellectual atheist, publishing some forty works on atheism and often being described as atheism's foremost "evangelist." Flew also regularly engaged leading Christian apologists in debates concerning the existence of God, the resurrection of Jesus, and life after death. We can only imagine the pain this had to cause his Christian parents, who were giving their lives in

---

* Antony Flew, *There Is a God* (New York: HarperOne, 2007), 15.

Christian ministry. We can only imagine how they continued to pray for their son.

In 2007, I was returning from India and was changing planes in New York. During the brief layover I walked into an airport bookstore to find some reading material for the final flight home. While browsing in the philosophy section, a book caught my eye: *There Is a God: How the World's Most Notorious Atheist Changed His Mind* by (you guessed it!) Antony Flew. I was stunned! I bought the book and read the whole thing on my flight back to Kansas City. It's probably the best apologetic work I've ever read on defending the existence of God. But it's more than just an argument for the existence of God; it is a fascinating autobiographical story of Flew's long, slow journey from atheism to belief in God.

Antony Flew is now eighty-five years old, and his parents have long since died. But their prayers live on—prayers that have now been answered. The strange and wonderful thing is, Antony Flew will probably end up doing more to bring people to belief in God through his late-in-life conversion following a lifetime of atheism than if he had followed his father into Christian ministry. I'm not suggesting that God was responsible for Antony Flew's atheism—I don't believe that—but I am suggesting that this is a marvelous example of God working all things together for good. I suspect Antony Flew's Methodist parents would agree.

How bad a day was it for Reverend and Mrs. Flew when their son announced that he had become an atheist? Could it perhaps have been the worst day of their lives? But that wasn't the end of the story. Antony Flew's parents did not live to see the answer to their prayers, but their prayers have been answered nonetheless, and in some strange mystical way we really can't understand right now, I believe that this couple will one day indeed rejoice. They will laugh with joy, they will give praise to their God, and they will shake their heads as they wonder and marvel over the incredible power of God to turn their story around.

Could it be people like Reverend and Mrs. Flew whom the writer of Hebrews is referring to in Hebrews 11 when he writes, "These all died in faith, not having received the promises, but having seen them afar off were assured of them"?[14]

In this life we will have some bad days. Some may be so bad that recovery seems impossible, but all things are possible to him who believes. On the worst day of your life, perhaps the best thing you can do is remember this promise: "All things work together for good," and dare to believe that this too will work out for good and that somehow everything is going to be all right. Remember, your times are in God's hand. He is the artist who has promised to weave all things in such a way that in the end your story will truly be a story of beauty, a work of art, God's masterpiece that can never be marred or touched, His beautiful tapestry of grace.

NOTES

5. Nehemiah 8:10
6. 1 Peter 5:8
7. James 1:2–4
8. Matthew 2:6;
Acts 7:10
9. Acts 26:2
10. James 1:3
11. 1 Peter 1:7
12. Habakkuk 2:4;
Romans 1:17;
Galatians 3:11;
Hebrews 10:38
13. 1 John 5:4
14. Proverbs 24:10
15. Luke 22:31
16. 1 Corinthians 10:13
17. Luke 22:32
18. James 1:3
19. James 1:4
20. Psalm 84:11
21. James 1:5

4—Get a Word From God

1. 1 Samuel 30:8
2. Romans 10:17
3. Matthew 14:29
4. John 4:24
5. Hebrews 4:12
6. Psalm 118:17
7. John 12:19
8. Psalm 27:13
9. Acts 16:5

5—Reorient Your Vision

1. 1 Samuel 30:8
2. James 1:6–8
3. Psalm 56:9

4. Genesis 39:2
5. Deuteronomy 28:13
6. Joshua 1:8
7. Psalm 35:27
8. John 10:10
9. 1 Corinthians 15:57
10. 2 Corinthians 2:14
11. Proverbs 25:11
12. Job 39:28–29
13. Isaiah 40:31
14. Ecclesiastes 1:2–9
15. Matthew 12:35

6—Regain Your Passion

1. 1 Samuel 30:16
2. Ephesians 6:12
3. Psalm 139:22
4. Matthew 25:41
5. Revelation 20:10
6. 1 John 3:8
7. Ephesians 4:26
8. John 11
9. John 11:35
10. John 11:33
11. John 11:38
12. John 11:43
13. 1 Thessalonians 4:16–17
14. Psalm 20:4, emphasis added
15. Psalm 37:4, emphasis added
16. Matthew 15:28, emphasis added
17. Mark 11:24
18. John 15:7, emphasis added
19. Isaiah 51:23
20. Luke 10:19

7—Attack!

1. 1 Samuel 30:17
2. 2 Corinthians 10:4
3. Ephesians 6:17
4. Revelation 1:16; 19:15
5. Matthew 4:1–11
6. Judges 3:16
7. Philippians 2:9–10
8. Philippians 3:21
9. Revelation 12:11
10. Leviticus 17:11
11. Genesis 4:10
12. Hebrews 9:22
13. Matthew 17:21
14. 2 Chronicles 20:1–30
15. Acts 16:23–34
16. 1 Corinthians 2:7–8
17. 1 Corinthians 1:20–25
18. 1 Corinthians 2:1–8
19. 2 Corinthians 2:14
20. Colossians 2:15

8—Recover All

1. 1 Samuel 30:18
2. Genesis 1:1
3. Genesis 3:15
4. John 12:12–16
5. Deuteronomy 21:23
6. Galatians 3:13–14
7. Colossians 1:19–20
8. Acts 3:18
9. Acts 3:19–21
10. 1 John 5:4–5
11. Isaiah 28:16
12. Ephesians 3:20–21

9—Celebrate Recovery

1. 1 Samuel 30:20
2. 1 Corinthians 2:9
3. Psalm 30:11–12
4. Isaiah 61:2
5. Genesis 50:19–21
6. Romans 5:20–21

10—Give to Others

1. Acts 13:22
2. 1 Samuel 30:16
3. Jude 12–13
4. Judges 14:14

Conclusion—
A Tapestry of Grace

1. Romans 8:28
2. Psalm 31:14–15
3. Genesis 1:1
4. 1 Thessalonians 2:18
5. Deuteronomy 30:19
6. Ecclesiastes 9:11; Luke 10:31
7. 1 Corinthians 8:3
8. Matthew 7:23
9. 1 Corinthians 13
10. Romans 8:18
11. Romans 8:19–25
12. Matthew 10:30
13. Romans 8:38–39
14. Hebrews 11:13

FREE NEWSLETTERS
TO HELP EMPOWER YOUR LIFE

Why subscribe today?

☐ **DELIVERED DIRECTLY TO YOU.** All you have to do is open your inbox and read.

☐ **EXCLUSIVE CONTENT.** We cover the news overlooked by the mainstream press.

☐ **STAY CURRENT.** Find the latest court rulings, revivals, and cultural trends.

☐ **UPDATE OTHERS.** Easy to forward to friends and family with the click of your mouse.

CHOOSE THE E-NEWSLETTER THAT INTERESTS YOU MOST:

- Christian news
- Daily devotionals
- Spiritual empowerment
- And much, much more

SIGN UP AT: **http://freenewsletters.charismamag.com**

8178

Become part of our community and gain strength
through the lives of others who are learning to
succeed through trials.

Join the conversation today at...

www.whattodoontheworstdayofyourlife.com